INVEST IN LIVING

HOME-MADE BUTTER, CHEESE AND YOGHURT

by

MAGGIE BLACK

EP Publishing Limited

Acknowledgements

The author's special thanks are due to Quainton Dairy, Pitchcott Hill Farm, Pitchcott, Nr. Aylesbury and its staff whose knowledge and help have given this book its substance.

The author and publisher also owe thanks to the following for reference and test materials, and for illustrations:

National Dairy Council
Chr. Hansen Laboratory Ltd
Akzo Chemie (UK) Ltd
Messrs. Fullwood and Bland Ltd
Butter Information Council
Taunton Cider Company Limited
Walls (Ice Cream) Limited
Mrs Carol Macartney
Miss Margaret Leach

Jacket photograph: John Harris.

Left to right: cheese moulds, home-made butter, Colwick cheese, York cheese, Russian Easter cheese, small-holder cheeses.

The *Invest in Living* Series

© EP Publishing Ltd 1977, 1979

ISBN 0 7158 0453 7

Published by EP Publishing Ltd, East Ardsley, Wakefield, West Yorkshire, 1977. Reprinted 1977, 1979

Text set in 11/12 pt Univers, printed by photolithography, and bound in Great Britain by G. Beard & Son Ltd, Brighton.

Contents

A Note on Milk for Cheeses, Butter and Yoghurt

Milk consists of water containing floating fat globules, and with other substance dissolved in it such as milk sugar or lactose (about 5%), casein (about 3%) and albumin ($\frac{1}{2}$%). These last two are milk proteins. Milk is also rich in calcium and vitamins, and in minerals vital to our health, as well as holding bacteria, some good and others which may be harmful.

The amount of fat in milk varies a good deal. Jersey and Guernsey cows give milk with more fat than other breeds, and the fat globules in their milk are larger. This is a help in butter-making since the cream is more easily separated from the milk. The butter is a deeper yellow colour too.

Other factors besides the breed of cow decide the amount of fat in cows' milk. The length of time the cow has been giving milk is one. The time of year is another. There is more milk to be had for cheese and butter-making in spring and summer, but milk is richer in late summer and autumn than in early spring.

Milk drains better in summer; that is, in warm weather. This is important, especially in making soft cheese. In fact it is wise to think of home cheese and butter-making as a summer craft. It is expensive to make either in the winter when milk is scarcer, and the dairying room or rooms (page 9) must be kept warm, at 18° − 21°C (65° − 70°F). Both cheeses and butter made in summer can be stored for use in winter-time.

If you do make cheeses or butter in winter, let the milk stand for 12−24 hours before using it, give rennet slightly longer stirring, and watch the temperature of the room carefully.

Milk for cheese, butter or yoghurt must be absolutely clean, and must all be of the same quality. Milk supplied commercially or from a large farm is nearly always pasteurised to make it so. If you use milk from a small herd, or from a house cow or goat, strain it into a scalded sterile pail or bowl as soon as it comes from the shed. Then, if you have any doubts about it, pasteurise it to 63°C (145°F) and cool it quickly to the temperature you want.

Goats' milk should be aerated by pouring it from one scalded container to another two or three times. This improves the flavour of cheeses made from it a good deal, especially soft cheeses.

All milk used for soft cheeses must be fresh. Sour milk makes dry, hard cheeses.

Your Own Dairy Foods

Making your own butter, cheeses and yoghurt is one of the most satisfying crafts to pursue. You can cut costs, while giving your family all the goodness which natural dairy foods provide. At the same time, you will have a hobby which is both interesting and creative. Certainly, if you can get plentiful supplies of milk, either from your own cow or goat or through a local dairy or farmer, you should take the chance to make your own dairy products.

All these dairy foods are delicious to eat. They add flavour and interest to any cooked dish, especially to plain meats, vegetables and puddings. Butter on jacket potatoes, for instance, macaroni cheese, yoghurt enriching a goulash or as a tangy, creamy dessert on its own!

If you make your own products, you can create just the flavour and texture you like. This way, you will give all your cooking, for the family or for guests, the personal touch which makes it original and good.

Its health value will be 'lifted' too. These dairy foods are packed with nutrients, especially good for children. Cheese, for instance, is one of our best all-round foods. It is rich in protein, the type of food essential for life, and it holds plenty of calcium, vitamins, and the fat we all need (even slimmers) to keep us warm. The only food it does not supply directly is carbohydrate—the sugar which gives quick energy— and we get that from the bread we eat with it.

Butter and yoghurt are among our best all-purpose foods too. We can use them raw or cooked, at any time of the day, for any kind of meal, and for both savoury and sweet dishes. So, like cheese, they are in a very real sense 'convenience' foods.

Cheese, in particular, is an almost perfect 'convenience' food, with extra value for old people. It makes the light yet nourishing meals they need and enjoy most. It is easy to cut and to chew; anyone who can use a spoon can have a high-protein meal. It is compact to carry, easy to handle and store. It keeps well, much longer than most protein foods, even if stored on a shelf or in a larder instead of a refrigerator. So it is a first-class standby for anyone who cannot go shopping easily, or who does not get in supplies often.

If you want good quality, cheeses are certainly cheaper if you make them yourself. When you take a firm block of well-flavoured cheese from its mould, you will have more than a sense of achievement. You will know that it has cost little more than the price of the milk; a spoonful of 'starter' and rennet, a small quantity of fuel and cleaning materials, that's all. Quite likely, you will not have had to buy any special equipment at first, either.

Fresh, soft cheeses are ideal 'make-at-home' products. Purchased ones go bad within a few days of being bought, and must therefore be used quickly. So it is really more practical to make one yourself when you need it.

Yoghurt probably makes an even better food for young children than cheese, since its milk proteins may be easier to digest. As a bonus, it is better for their teeth, since it does not stick to them. Leaving aside the myths about yoghurt's health-giving properties, it really is a wonderful food for both children and adults because it contains almost all the valuable nutrients in milk, and little else. This makes it ideal for growing children; yet it is good for a slimming diet too, provided you stick to a low-fat type, without sweetening or added fruit.

Yoghurt is much cheaper if made at home. You can save as much as a third of its cost by making it yourself. You need no special equipment, nor even much skill, to create this luxuriously creamy product; and a good

many people prefer it to real cream in this figure-conscious age!

There is, however, no substitute for real butter, either for its flavour or its role in making rich, melting pastry and cakes, fillings, frostings and sauces. Butter is the queen of dairy products; even a touch of it adds grace to any dish. So it is well worth making, not only for economy but to have more of it to use.

In fact, by making all three dairy products, you will get generous supplies economically, which you can use alone or to enhance your cooking generally. Besides this, you will have a sense of achievement. A firm golden block of butter, a well-shaped and clean-tasting cheese, a glass of snowy yoghurt as sharp as you choose to make it—these will be products you can take pride in, and enjoy offering to your family and your friends.

A Table of English Cheeses

Cheese	Notes on Manufacture	Traditional shape and size	Remarks
HARD PRESSED, SCALDED CHEESE			
English Cheddar	A fairly hard, pressed cheese, scalded at 36°C – 45°C. Rich and excellent for cooking or eating raw. The most famous English cheese, known world wide.	10" high 14" diameter	Close and buttery in texture. Full, nutty rich flavour, yet not overstrong.
English Cheshire	Lower scalding – to only (32°C – 35°C) – avoids too hard a curd. Cheshire ripens in four weeks. A red colour is sometimes introduced by adding a harmless vegetable colouring.	13" high 11" diameter	Loose and crumbly in texture. Its keen, tangy flavour is often said to be due to the salty soil in Cheshire on which the cattle graze. Cheshire cheese can be red, white or blue. (see below)
Derby	The curd is cut into $\frac{1}{2}$" cubes and is still quite moist at milling. It ripens in six months.	5" high 14" diameter	A beautiful white cheese with a smooth texture and soft, mild flavour. The rare Sage Derby gets extra flavour by being impregnated with the extract pressed out of finely-chopped sage leaves.
Double Gloucester	The manufacture of Double Gloucester is very close to Cheddar. Double Gloucester ripens in four to six months.	4" high 15" diameter	Close and smooth in texture, straw-coloured or light red. It has a mellow, fairly pungent flavour.
Leicester	The curd in the vat is drained under pressure from weighted wooden racks. Very finely milled. The cheese ripens in two months.	4" high 18" diameter	Leicester Cheese is a rich red colour. Mild to taste. Soft, crumbly and flaky in texture. It is shaped like a millstone.
LIGHTLY PRESSED AND SCALDED CHEESE			
Caerphilly	The new cheese is soaked in brine for 24 hours after a day's light pressing. Then dried and stored. It ripens in fourteen days.	3" high 9" diameter	A creamy white cheese with a mild delicate flavour and semi-smooth texture.
Lancashire	Part of the previous day's curd is mixed with part of the current day's. This produces a cheese with a loose, soft body. The curd is drained in cloth bundles on wooden racks and milled as fine as chopped suet.	8" high 13" diameter	Crumbly and fairly soft, with a clean and mild flavour. It is especially famous for its toasting quaiities.
White Wensleydale	Only about 1 pint of starter is used to 100 gallons of milk. The milled curd is packed into unlined metal moulds and left to drain for 1 to 2 hours before gentle pressing. It ripens in twelve to fourteen days.	6" high 8" diameter	This celebrated cheese was first produced in the Middle Ages by Monks of Jervaulx Abbey on the River Ure. The lingering creamy sweet-tasting flavour of Wensleydale is unique.
BLUE VEINED CHEESE	The blue-green veining in Blue Stilton and Blue Wensleydale is a harmless mould which grows in air spaces in the loosely packed curd. This is encouraged by the circulation of air from outside. The growth of this mould is essential to develop the clean, piquant flavour of a blue cheese.		
Blue Stilton	The curd is cut; ladled into shallow sinks lined with perforated trays; left overnight. It is then broken very carefully by hand into small pieces. Salted and packed gently into hoops. The hoops are drained on calico squares laid on boards; the cloths and boards being changed daily for 10 days. Then the hoop is removed. The sides of the cheese scraped, and the scrapings used to fill the crevices. The cheese is bandaged and replaced in the hoops. It is turned and re-bandaged daily until a 'coat' forms and white mould begins to grow on the surface. Blue veins form in cracks in the cheese body. To allow them to form properly the cheese must ripen very slowly. Aeration encourages the growth of this mould and may be increased by piercing the cheese with wires.	9" high 8" diameter	Stilton is sometimes called the 'king of cheeses'. It has a wrinkled brown coat, a creamy-white, blue-veined body. Its taste is superb – rich and 'edgy'.
Blue Wensleydale	Similar to Stilton but the soft curds are drained on racks. Very light pressure is applied to the curds in the hoops.	6" high 8" diameter	Gets its honeyed taste from the limestone in the soil of the Yorkshire Ure Valley.
Blue Cheshire	Creamy-yellow with banded blue streaks, it gets its colour from penicillinum glaucum.		Flavoured by the minerals in the grazing, Blue Cheshire, like White Cheshire, cannot be made anywhere else.

Your Dairy

This book is for people who want to make butter, cheeses or yoghurt on a small scale, for use at home. It is for anyone who wants to use the surplus milk of a single house cow or goat, or who can get good milk supplies easily from a local farmer or dairy, for domestic use. If you plan to make butter, cheeses or yoghurt on this scale, you will probably not use more than 15 litres (3 gallons) of milk at a time.

You can handle this quantity quite easily in any normal-sized room. Ideally, it should be separate from your kitchen. However, if you have no other space available, you must ensure that your kitchen is scrupulously clean, especially if you make bread or process soft fruit there; the yeasts can infect cheese and yoghurt curds, and spoil your products. You will also need a separate storage area near your 'dairy' where you can keep tools and cheese moulds, and also 'cure' any hard cheeses on open-rack shelves.

The room you use as your 'dairy' need not be large, but it should contain a cooker and a sink (preferably a low-level one into which you can hoist buckets easily), and a big work table. There should also be space to stack a few big pans and buckets. A refrigerator is essential for butter, soft cheeses and yoghurt, and a home freezer if you have one is a great help too. (Ideas for varying and using soft cheeses are given on page 29 to help you if you have no freezer.)

Butter or cheese making on any larger scale than 15 litres per session, requires a good deal more space than this. If you want to make them for community use or for sale, you should have a proper dairy, outside the house. It should be tiled, if possible, and have a concrete or tiled floor, for easy cleaning. In the room where you actually make the butter and cheese, there must be enough space to stand churns, and somewhere to put a cream separator if possible (see page 45). In a separate area, where you will salt, bathe and brush down any hard cheeses you make, you will need a brine-tub, and a metal work surface on which to coat your cheeses with fat, wax or cornflour without any problem of lasting smears or smells. A home freezer is almost essential, too, if you want to keep butter, soft cheeses or yoghurt to market at intervals or for eating over a period.

Even in a small kitchen or 'dairy' where you make butter, cheeses and yoghurt just for family use, try to have tiles or stout lino on the floor and gloss-painted walls. Both the room and the equipment you use must be scrupulously clean to prevent harmful bacteria spoiling your milk. The milk itself must be pure and clean too; dirty milk does not drain properly. See the note on milk, on page 4.

The equipment you will need as a 15-litre (3-gallon) butter or cheese-maker is simple, and need not be costly (see page 16). In fact, much of it can come from your own home kitchen. But the basic items should be as good as you can afford. Old battered pans or cracked jugs shelter bacteria. For this reason, everything you use in your dairy, especially equipment from your kitchen, must be sterilised before you use it for dairy work (see page 18).

Not all bacteria are harmful. When you keep a separate room just for a dairy, many things in it will be covered with the minute organisms called *Streptococcus Lactis* (*Strep. Lactis,* for short). Like harmful yeasts, they get into the milk, and work on it. You should encourage them. They are the cheese-maker's best friends because, in fact, they make the cheese.

They cannot do this, however, if the room is too cold or too hot for them. After cleanliness, the most important thing to ensure, in any dairy, is that its temperature is right. The place where you make your cheeses should be kept at a fairly even temperature of about 21°C (70°F). If the temperature falls much below this, or if the curd is exposed to draughts, it will not drain properly, and the cheeses will be soggy.

When you are making butter, the room should be a little cooler than this, somewhere between 10° and 16°C (50° and 60°F). The place where you 'cure' and store your hard cheeses should be kept at this temperature too. If the room is too warm, an electric fan will usually cool it down.

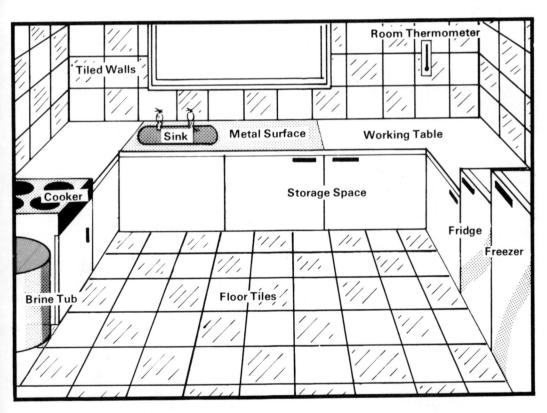

Cheeses You Can Make

What, actually, is cheese?

When milk becomes more acid than usual, its solid particles such as the milk proteins, stick together as a soft mass like a thick custard, called curd. A good deal of the water in the milk, with some of the milk's other substances dissolved in it, is separate from the curd and can be drained off. This liquid is called whey. The whey can be separated and drained from the curd more easily if they are heated together to a temperature over 15°C (60°F).

Cheese is just a curd, made with acid, which has been drained of its whey. You can eat this curd just as it is, as a fresh soft cheese, or you can press it in moulds to squeeze out the whey completely, and so make the cheese last longer.

Cheese is, therefore, essentially a very simple product to make.

However, there are a number of 'variable' factors which make some kinds of cheeses more complicated to make than just pressing curd in a mould. Cheeses vary according to the cow's pasture, the weather and the season, and even the time of day she is milked. It will also vary according to:

- whether the milk is just from one milking or has the previous evening's milk added to it
- whether the milk is skimmed, or partly skimmed, or has had cream added
- what means have been used to make the milk more acid
- how warm the milk is when the curd forms, and how acid it is
- whether the milk is then heated further (scalded) to make the curd more condensed, with more free whey
- whether the cheese is pressed, and if so, how much, for how long
- whether the cheese has salt or other flavourings added
- whether moulds are encouraged to grow in the cheese, as they are in 'blue' cheeses.

Any of these factors will affect the milk quite differently in different places. Cheese made in Gloucestershire may turn out quite differently from cheese made in Somerset even though the same processes have been used from first to last.

Luckily, modern cheese scientists now know a good deal about the way the 'variables' work, and have given us equipment for controlling them. For instance, we know that, to make some kinds of cheeses, the curd should be scalded at under 38°C (100°F), and we can use a modern dairy thermometer to tell us when this temperature is reached. In fact there are standard modern recipes for most cheeses which will 'work', given care, under almost any circumstances.

They work partly because most milk today varies much less than in the past. Almost all our cattle get some artificial feeding. Most milk processed commercially, and any large-scale farmer's, is mixed from several different herds, and pasteurised; and government regulations demand that it should meet a certain quality standard. So if you, as a 15-litre (3-gallon) cheese-maker, use bought milk, you can follow any standard recipe with confidence.

However, if you use the milk of your own cow or goat, you may still have to adapt the recipes by trial and error until you find a formula which works for you. Your cow's milk has its own individual character, and the standard processes may not suit it at all. Equally, some procedures which the text-books condemn may make marvellous cheeses.

A good many cheeses are really outside the scope of an average small-scale cheese-maker. The traditional British hard cheeses, for instance, are quite complicated to make, and are too large for one person to handle easily, if full-sized. Look back at the Table of English Cheeses. Even the smallest, Caerphilly, will weigh about 4 kg (8 lb.) which means handling at least 40 litres (8 gallons) of milk—just for one cheese! Even lifting the milk pans on to the stove is quite hard work, and some of the equipment needed is massive.

These cheeses are now made commercially in smaller sizes; but they are made under specially controlled conditions, to give them the flavour and aroma of the large, more slowly matured cheeses. If you make them at home, they are likely to disappoint you.

So will many of the well-known foreign semi-soft cheeses. We do not have the right conditions or 'starters' to make most of them. However, several cheeses—more than most people think —can be made at home very successfully. They include fresh and fermented ones, old types and new, soft ones and pressed types. These are described below so that you can decide which to experiment with first. The terms explained will help you, too, when you come to the techniques of cheese-making in the next section.

Cheeses to Make at Home
Soft Cheeses

All soft cheeses still contain a good deal of whey. So, unlike cheeses which are pressed and dry, they do not keep long. Home-made ones are nearly all fresh cheeses, unripened and unfermented—that is, bacteria have not been given time to grow and work on them—and are ready for eating as soon as they are made. Some, though not all, are bland, and can be used in sweet dishes as well as savoury ones.

These cheeses are usually grouped according to their butterfat content (how much fat they contain). In England, there are six grades:

skimmed milk soft cheese (less than 2% fat)

low fat soft cheese (2%–10% fat)

medium fat soft cheese (10%–20% fat)

'simple cream' cheese (45% fat)

full fat soft cheese (20%–45% fat)

'cream' or 'cream-hearted' cheese (55% fat)

cream cheese (45%–65% fat)

'double cream' cheese (60% fat)

double cream cheese (at least 65% fat)

'triple cream' cheese (75% fat)

In case you want to make French-style soft cheeses, here are the grades:

'thin' cheese made with skimmed milk

Another way to group these cheeses is according to the kind of acid used to make their curd (see page 10 above). Most fresh soft cheeses are 'lactic' cheeses. They are made with untreated or raw milk. If this milk is kept warm, the minute *Strep. Lactis* organisms in the milk convert the milk sugar (lactose) into lactic acid. We can taste it, and say that the milk has soured. Heat-treated milk, e.g. pasteurised milk, has had its *Strep. Lactis* destroyed, so it must be put back, by using what we call a 'starter' (a culture containing the organisms) to sour and curdle the milk. There is a 'starter' recipe on page 19.

When *Strep. Lactis* curdles milk, the milk is soured naturally. But we can also curdle milk by using enzymes such as rennet. Calf's rennet is the curdling agent most often used, but it is not the only one. There are vegetables and herbs which 'set' milk; or one can use lemon juice, vinegar, or an acid such as cream of tartar.

Making yoghurt is another way of curdling milk. Minute organisms not unlike *Strep. Lactis* do it; their 'official' scientific names are *Lactobacillus bulgaricus* and *acidophillus,* plus *Streptococcus thermophilus.*

Yoghurts and the products you can make with them, including the soft yoghurt cheeses, are described on pages 54–71.

Lactic and renneted soft cheeses can be made at home very easily, and you can vary them in a great many different ways to suit yourself. You can:

- skim or partly skim the milk
- add a little, or a lot, of single or double cream
- add butter instead of cream
- add other flavourings such as herbs or wine
- add other foods such as chopped nuts or fruit
- leave the curd to drain naturally
- make the curd firmer by cutting it up and heating it gently
- make the curd more solid still, by pressing it under a light weight.

All these methods make slightly different types of soft cheese.

Here are some types you can try:

Curd cheese, low fat, medium or full fat

The basic lactic soft cheese. It is slightly sharp in flavour, being soured and curdled naturally. Salt is usually added but no other flavouring. Curd cheese is often called 'pot' cheese, 'clabber' cheese or 'farmer's' cheese. Farmer's cheese has less whey drained out of it than the other two forms of curd cheese. It is broken up more finely, and is put into a mould.

Cream cheese

Real cream cheese is usually a renneted cheese. Naturally soured cream can taste bitter; and thick cream just left to firm up, and moulded before it sours, is not really cheese. Cream cheese has salt added to make it last a day or two; otherwise it would 'go off' very quickly.

Cottage cheese

Renneted and heat-treated cheese. Tricky to make, compared with curd cheeses. It is usually more easily and cheaply bought than made at home. Bland in flavour, although a little salt is added. Made with skimmed milk with a little added cream.

Crowdie

Curdled with a 'starter' and heated. Can be made with skimmed or full milk. Sharp-flavoured, with a pasty texture. Keeps for 5–6 days, with added salt.

Cambridge or York cheese

Full fat, renneted cheese, whitish in colour with a band of gold in the centre. Less sharp than a curd or other lactic cheese. Has salt added. Creamy in texture. Usually set in an oblong mould.

Colwick cheese

Full fat, renneted cheese, heated. Is an attractive 'bun' shaped with curled-over edges. Slightly acid flavour. Salted. Smooth in texture.

Coulommier cheese

Renneted cheese, turned during draining. Mild in flavour, and medium soft. Has the best texture of all soft smooth cheeses. Only lightly salted.

Russian Easter cheese

Usually called Pashka. Lactic curd cheese with cream and eggs added, also dried fruit and nuts. Set in a pyramid or flower-pot mould. One of the simplest and best of the hundreds of sweet dessert soft cheeses.

Sage cheese

Cream cheese with sage and spinach leaves added. Lightly pressed. One of the oldest English herb cheeses. Herb-flavoured and slightly less oily in texture than plain cream cheeses.

Recipes for all these cheeses, except cottage cheese, are given on pages 21–28. (For yoghurt soft cheeses, see page 71.)

Hard Cheeses

Many books, and eager cheese-makers too, will supply recipes for making Cheddar, Wensleydale and other semi-hard cheeses in large or small sizes. Given care, patience and effort, most of these recipes work. But, unless you have farm-style outhouses, and are prepared to go to some expense to do cheese-making on a large scale, avoid them. In general, the larger and older semi-hard cheeses are, the better they are, up to the time they are fully mature. To gain their full, rich flavour, they need to be full-sized and stored for some weeks or months. Then they supply more cheese of a single kind than the average family needs.

High quality Farmhouse English cheeses are still made on certain farms. They are made and matured under controlled conditions, and are quite widely available. The kitchen cheese-maker is wiser to buy a piece from one of these properly matured cheeses than to make her own. She can then give her family varied types of cheese, usually of better quality than she can make at home.

There is one exception. Anyone with a household cow or goat, or who can lay hands on a bulk supply of 15–20 litres (3–4 gallons) of milk easily and

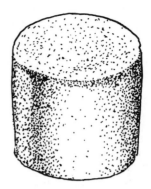

cheaply can make Smallholder Cheese. This is an attractive semi-hard cheese, not unlike Cheddar or Cheshire (depending on whether cow's or goat's milk is used), usually made in sizes easily coped with by a normal householder and family. It is an excellent cheese to try if you want to understand the basic processes of making all semi-hard and firm cheeses, since, in essence, they are all made in the same way. Smallholder's Cheese is renneted and 'pitched', has salt added, is 'milled', moulded and pressed like the larger semi-hard cheeses. When ready, its flavour is mild but definitely 'cheesy', and its texture is smooth and firm. The recipe is on page 41, and the terms used to describe it above are explained there too.

Making Soft Cheeses

Most of us have made soft cheeses of one kind or another. Usually, it is 'pot' or 'farmer's' cheese (page 13), made without a starter from naturally soured milk. The method of making it is simple. When the sour milk forms a curd, you tip it gently into a piece of muslin, or similar cloth with a fairly close weave. You tie the ends of the cloth together, to form a bag; then you hang it over a sink, or lay it in a sieve placed over a basin, so that the curd can drain. You may fork over the curd from time to time, to make it release its whey and have a creamier texture; and you probably add salt and perhaps a little cream or butter and herb flavouring to it. When it is as firm as you want it, you scrape it out of the cloth and use it.

This could hardly be easier. The only thing to watch out for is that naturally sour milk very soon goes 'bad' after it has curded. Other organisms take over from the *Strep. Lactis* which sour the milk (page 12); they make it putrid, so that, instead of the slightly sharp but pleasant acid taste of naturally sour milk, its flavour is bitter. However, if you can process the milk at the right moment before this happens, you can make an attractive fresh-tasting soft salad or dessert cheese with no trouble.

In one way, the lactic soft cheeses made with a starter and the renneted soft cheeses are even easier to make; one does not wait for the milk to sour naturally, so it gets no chance to turn unpleasantly bitter. There are a few more steps in the method of making these cheeses and you will need a few items of equipment besides the cloth, sieve and basin and fork, but these should present no problems.

Equipment

For reliable stockists of all the home dairy equipment suggested in this book, see page 72.

The basic equipment you will need for making all lactic soft cheeses is:
 a hair or nylon strainer or sieve, 15–20 cm (6–8 in.) across
 a pan to heat the milk in
 a thermometer
 close-textured cotton cloth
 string
 a fork or spoon for scraping down the curd
 a ladle.

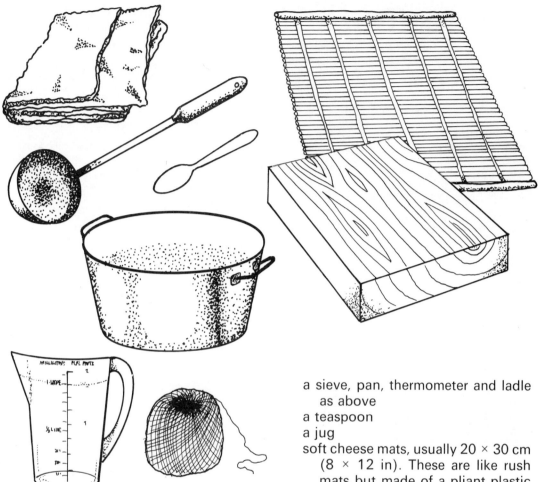

Choose a pan big enough to lift without risk of spilling the milk, and which can be placed over direct heat. It should have two lug handles rather than a single long one; that is, a casserole-style pan is better than a saucepan-style one. If you can, get a floating dairy thermometer; it can be left in the milk to tell you the rate at which it is heating, and it records low temperatures more accurately than a jelly or fat thermometer.

For making renneted soft cheeses, you will need:

a sieve, pan, thermometer and ladle as above

a teaspoon

a jug

soft cheese mats, usually 20 × 30 cm (8 × 12 in). These are like rush mats but made of a pliant plastic material

soft cheese boards, usually 22.5 × 32.5 cm (9 × 13 in.). These are made of a light, absorbent material, like softboard

a mould for the type of cheese you are making.

Use a metal jug and get good quality mats and boards which will stand up to being boiled. Coulommier moulds can be used for cream (and Colwick) cheeses, but Cambridge cheese needs an oblong mould and Pashka a pyramid one. (You can see these on the cover.) A mould for

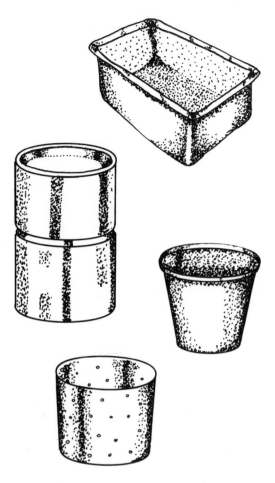

the yeasts used in bread making (page 8 above).

All equipment must be sterilised before you use it. Boil metal and boilable polythene tools. Sterilise jars and bottles with boiling water or by oven heating as you would do before bottling fruit. After using your equipment, wash it thoroughly before storing it. Never use soap or a detergent on wooden equipment, or on cheese mats. Simply scrub them, using very hot water. You can wash metal and

Cambridge cheese can be made by piercing small round holes in a 12.5 × 10 cm (5 × 4 in.) foil dish at 5 cm (2 in.) intervals. A rigid polythene flowerpot with several holes in the bottom makes an adequate Pashka mould, although a proper cheese mould with holes in the sides is better. A few other items, such as muslin, bowls and a small chopping knife, are needed for certain cheeses. They are listed in the recipes.

Caring for your equipment is important. Dirty or battered equipment may hold bacteria which will spoil your cheese in much the same way as

polythene equipment in detergent, but be sure that you rinse it off very thoroughly.

Store your equipment away from dust and where flies cannot reach it. Keep bottles of rennet and starter culture in a cool, dark place until you need them. Label bottles very clearly in large letters; they often look similar and can easily be mistaken for each other.

Starters

If you use pasteurised, sterilised or UHT milk for making soft cheeses, the milk's own *Strep. Lactis* has been destroyed, and must be replaced in order to make the milk curdle. You get it from what we call a 'starter culture', a substance (usually liquid) already teeming with it.

Raw milk, and milk used for renneted cheeses, do not strictly need a 'starter' injection of *Strep. Lactis* to make a curd start forming. But using a starter gives the cheese flavour and aroma, and a firmer curd. So many cheeses are made with both a starter and rennet.

There are several ways to obtain live starter culture. You can buy it frozen or dried from a laboratory (page 72) or you can make your own. In fact, when you buy it, you should always use some of the bought culture to make more culture of your own before you use it to make cheese. *Strep. Lactis* and similar organisms do not live long once the containers are opened and you must keep breeding them if you want to save the nuisance and cost of buying a fresh supply for every cheese-making session.

There are two stages in making your own starter culture. The first is to **innoculate** sterile milk with the *Strep. Lactis* from a bottle of live starter culture. The second is to **incubate** the *Strep. Lactis* so that it grows and is active in the milk.

Buy at least your first lot of live cheese starter culture from a laboratory if you can.

To Innoculate Starter Culture

First, prepare some containers for sterile milk. Get strong glass bottles with well-fitting screw caps such as tonic water bottles. Wash them out with boiling water.

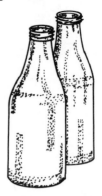

Boil the milk to be sterilised and cool it slightly. Pour it into the bottles until nearly full. Screw on the caps, then unscrew them half a turn. Place the

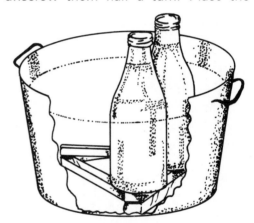

bottles on a rack, trivet or crumpled cloth in a deep pan. Fill the pan with hot water to the level of the milk in the bottles. Bring to the boil and simmer for one to two hours with a lid on the pan. Allow the milk to cool naturally, not by chilling. When quite cool, tighten the screw caps and place the bottles in the refrigerator until required. Use within five days.

If the milk turns brown during cooking, reduce the cooking time slightly when making the next batch. The brown milk can be used quite safely. If, however, the milk turns solid during sterilisation, it means that it was beginning to sour. Throw it away, wash out the bottles thoroughly and start again.

When the milk is prepared, get ready the following equipment:

    1 or more bottles of sterilised milk
    1 bottle of live starter culture
    a naked flame, e.g. the burner on a gas cooker.

Assemble the bottles and light the flame. This sterilises the air immediately around it. Shake the bottle of starter culture until the contents are liquid. Loosen the caps on both bottles. Pick up the caps in the crook of your little finger (not by putting a finger or

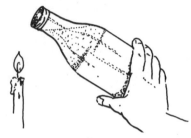

thumb inside). Waft the necks of the bottles through the flame, then quickly pour about one 5 ml spoon (one tea-

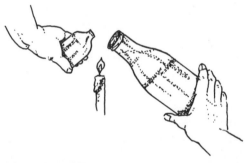

spoon) of starter culture into the sterilised milk, holding both bottles as near to the flame as possible. Stand the bottles on the table and replace the caps as quickly as possible. Shake the bottle(s) of sterilised milk to mix in the culture.

Put the original live starter culture on one side, ready to use for cheese-making.

To Incubate Starter Culture

Leave the bottle of sterilised milk innoculated with starter culture in a warm place for 8–12 hours. The temperature should be around 21°C (70°F). As soon as the milk 'sets' like curd, refrigerate it until required for use. Before using it, make a new batch of starter culture from it if necessary. Make at least two new bottles, one for use, the other for freezing if you have a freezer.

You can freeze the culture after innoculating it but before incubating it if you wish. Use a bottle of milk only half full. Store it frozen for two to three months if required. To use it, thaw it at room temperature, then incubate it as above.

With one or two very small differences, this is the way to innoculate and incubate yoghurt starter culture (page 56) as well as cheese starter culture; also, any other cultures you may want to use such as a 'blue mould' for making blue veined cheeses. A good laboratory, such as Chr. Hansen's of Reading will supply a complete list of their cultures. See page 72.

No starter culture lives for ever. Starter bacteria weaken and die as soon as they have consumed most of the nourishment the milk gives. As soon as the milk used for a starter culture begins to smell sourish, you must innoculate a new supply of sterile milk. Starter culture is only healthy while it has a clean, acid smell, is free from gas holes and shows no whey separating out. If you notice any of these features, throw the culture away, and incubate your second bottle.

Even healthy bacteria given a regular supply of new sterile milk to grow in, weaken after about two months. Cheese starter culture which takes longer than 12 hours to set is probably also weak and due for replacement.

Rennet

Cheese rennet is stronger than rennet bought at a chemist's. Various suppliers (page 72) package animal and vegetarian rennet for the home user. It should be kept in a cool, dry dark place, and used according to the manufacturer's instructions. Even then, it has a limited life, so do not buy too much at one time.

If you cannot get cheese rennet when you need it, you can use essence of rennet (junket rennet) but you will have to use three to six times the quantity suggested in the recipes.

Curd Cheese

Makes 1 kg (approx. 2 lb.) cheese
   from 5 litres (1 gallon) milk

Skimmed or whole milk
Starter
Salt (optional)

Equipment: pan, thermometer, 15 ml
   spoon (tablespoon), close-textured
   cotton cloth, string, bucket.

Heat the milk to 74°C (165°F). Let it cool to 32°C (90°F). Add 2 × 15 ml spoons (2 tablespoons) starter per 5 litres (1 gallon) milk. Stir in thoroughly. Cover and leave in a warm place for 12–18 hours or until a firm curd forms.

Scald a large square cloth for each 5 litres (1 gallon) of milk. Ladle the curd

When the cheese has the texture you want, add 15–25 g ($\frac{1}{2}$–1 oz.) salt per 500 g (1 lb.) curd for savoury use. Leave unsalted for using in cheese-cakes. Store in a refrigerator.

Quick Sour Milk Pot Cheese

$2\frac{1}{4}$ litres (2 quarts) sour milk
1 generous litre (1 quart) buttermilk
Single cream
Salt

Equipment: large saucepan, skimmer, muslin, string.

Put the sour milk and buttermilk in a saucepan and heat gently to scalding point. Remove from the heat and take off the curd with a skimmer. Place it in the muslin, draw up the corners and tie to enclose the curd. Hang up and allow to drain for one to two hours. Moisten the curd with cream and salt to taste, work well with the hands and form into small balls. Lay on a dish, cover and refrigerate until ready to serve. Eat within 24 hours.

into it. Gather up the corners to form a bag and hang over a bucket to drain. After six hours, scrape down any curd on the cloth into the main mass of curd, and hang up again. Repeat this process two or three times during the next 24–36 hours, replacing the cloth at least once.

22

Crowdie

Makes about 1 kg (2 lb.) cheese
from 5 litres (1 gallon) milk

Skimmed or full cream milk
Starter
Salt

Equipment: large pan or double
boiler, 15 ml spoon (tablespoon),
ladle, close-textured cotton cloth,
string, thermometer, bucket.

Heat the milk to 72°C (160°F). Cool
immediately to 27°C (80°F). Add 2 ×
15 ml spoons (2 tablespoons) starter
to each 5 litres (1 gallon) milk. Stir
thoroughly, cover and leave in a warm
place overnight or until a smooth solid
curd forms.

Slice the curd gently and heat it
to 38°C (100°F) very slowly, stirring
gently all the time. Keep the curd at
38°C (100°F) for 30 minutes.

Boil a large square cloth for each
5 litres (1 gallon) milk. Pour in the curds
and whey and hang up over a bucket to
drain. After a few hours, open the bags,
scrape down any curd on the cloth
and mix into the main mass. Re-hang.

Next day, boil fresh cloths and
scrape the curd into them. Re-hang.
A few hours later, scrape down as
before. If nearly the right consistency,
add salt to taste. Re-hang until the
cheese has the texture you want.
Pack into pots or plastic bags. Use
within five days or freeze.

Cream Cheese 1

Weight depends on whether double
or single cream is used

Double or single cream
Starter
Cheese rennet (with single cream)
Salt

Equipment: pan or double boiler,
15 ml spoon (tablespoon) 5 ml
spoon (teaspoon), close-textured
cotton cloth, string, bucket,
Cambridge cheese moulds.

Heat the cream very gently to 80°C
(175°F) then cool to 27°C (80°F). Add
1 × 15 ml spoon (1 tablespoon) starter
to each litre (1 quart) cream. Stir in
well, cover and leave in a warm place.
If using single cream, add 1 × 5 ml
spoon (1 teaspoon) rennet per litre
(1 quart) cream after two to three
hours. Boil cloths and moulds. After
8–12 hours, or when a firm curd has
formed, salt the cheese to taste and
hang in cloths to drain, like Curd
Cheese. Scrape down in the same way.
When the cheese has the texture and
flavour you wish, pack into moulds.
Store in a refrigerator. Use within five
days or freeze.

Cream Cheese 2

Weight depends on the additions
 used

375 ml ($\frac{3}{4}$ pt.) double or single cream
 (can be partly top of the milk)
1 × 5 ml spoon (1 teaspoon) starter
8 drops cheese rennet
Salt and pepper to taste or one of the
 following: a little chopped canned
 pineapple, drained, 1 × 5 ml spoon
 (1 teaspoon) sherry, chopped nuts

Equipment: pan, wooden spoon,
 5 ml spoon (teaspoon), butter
 muslin, two plates, weight.

Heat the cream very gently to 21°C
(70°F), stirring with the wooden spoon
occasionally. Stir in 1 × 5 ml spoon
(1 teaspoon) starter and eight drops
rennet. Cover with butter muslin and
leave in a warm place for 16 hours.
Pour off the whey carefully and season
to taste with either salt and pepper or
with one of the sweet additions.
When the flavouring has been worked
in, tie the curd in a tight bag of butter
muslin and place on a plate with
another, weighted plate on top. Leave
in a cool place for 48 hours before use.
Store in a refrigerator. Use within five
days or freeze.

Cambridge or York Cheese

Makes 2 × 480 g (approx. 1 lb.)
 cheeses from 7 litres (approx.
 1$\frac{1}{2}$ gallons) milk

7 litres (1$\frac{1}{2}$ gallons) full cream milk
1 × 5 ml spoon (1 teaspoon) starter

3 × 2.5 ml spoons (1$\frac{1}{2}$ teaspoons)
 cheese rennet
Annatto (or marigold petals or saffron
 infused in a little hot water to
 make the water deep gold)
Salt

Equipment: pan, polythene bowl,
 thermometer, 5 ml spoons
 (teaspoons), 1 litre jug, two oblong
 cheese moulds (see page 18), two
 soft cheese boards, two soft
 cheese mats, ladle, greaseproof
 paper.

Heat the milk to 68°C (155°F). Cool
immediately to 32°C (90°F). Stir in
1 × 5 ml spoon starter. Leave to ripen
for 20 minutes if desired.
 Dilute 3 × 2.5 ml spoons (1$\frac{1}{2}$ teaspoons) rennet in a scant 25 ml water.

Add to the milk and stir in thoroughly.
Transfer 2 litres (4 pt.) milk to a
polythene bowl. Add annatto or in-
fusion of herbs to give a light gold
colour.
 Cover both curds and leave for 30
minutes or until a firm curd forms.
During this time, boil boards, mats
and moulds for 10 minutes.
 Stand the moulds on the mats on
the boards. Ladle thin slices of white
curd into each mould until just over
one-third full. Cover with thin slices
of golden curd. Then fill moulds with
remaining white curd.

Cover with greaseproof paper. Leave the curd to drain for two to three days until the cheese is about 5 cm (2 in.) deep and fairly firm.

Remove from the moulds. Salt the surface of the cheese lightly and spread the salt. Wrap in greaseproof paper and store in a refrigerator for 24 hours before use. Use within a week or freeze in not larger than 100 g (4 oz.) portions.

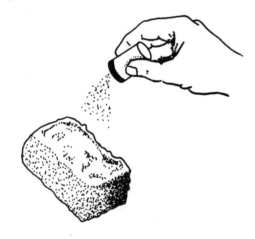

Colwick Cheese

Makes two cheeses per 5 litres
  (1 gallon) milk

5 litres (1 gallon) full cream milk
1 × 5 ml spoon (1 teaspoon) starter
3 × 2.5 ml spoons (1½ teaspoons)
  cheese rennet
25 g (1 oz.) salt
Double cream

Equipment: pan, thermometer, ladle,
  3 × 2.5 cm spoons (1 teaspoon),
  jug, one soft cheese mat, one soft
  cheese board, two cylindrical
  moulds 17.5 cm (7 in.) high and
  12.5 cm (5 in.) diameter, muslin,
  storage cartons.

Heat the milk to 68°C (155°F). Cool immediately to 32°C (90°F). Add 1 × 5 ml spoon (1 teaspoon) starter and ripen for 30 minutes if you wish. Add 3 × 2.5 ml spoons (1½ teaspoons) rennet diluted in a scant 25 ml water. Stir, reaching down to the bottom of the pan, for two minutes, then leave to stand for 30–40 minutes or until a firm curd forms.

Boil board, mat and muslin for 10 minutes. Boil moulds if possible. Place the mats on the boards and place the moulds on the mats. Line the moulds

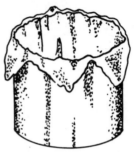

with muslin, letting it hang over the edges.

Slice the curd thinly and place in the moulds.

After one hour, pull the muslin upward and inward, drawing the curd from the sides of the mould. Knot firmly in the centre. Repeat the process several times during the next few hours, to produce curled-over edges and a depression in the middle. Leave for 24–48 hours.

When the curd is firm enough to handle, remove the mould. Peel off the

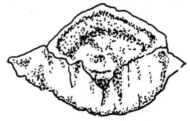

muslin carefully. Sprinkle with 25 g salt (for two cheeses) and leave to dry slightly. Place in cartons and store in refrigerator for seven days. Just before serving, whip the double cream and fill the hollow centres of the cheeses.

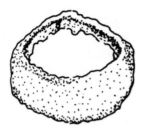

Coulommier Cheese

Makes three cheeses per 5 litres (1 gallon) milk

5 litres (1 gallon) full cream milk
1 or 2 × 2.5 ml spoons (1–2 teaspoons) starter
1 × 5 ml spoon (1 teaspoon) cheese rennet
25 g salt

Equipment: two soft cheese mats, 20 × 30 cm (8 × 12 in.), two soft cheese boards, 22.5 × 32.5 cm (9 × 13 in.), three Coulommier moulds, 1 × 4½ litre (10 pint) pan, metal ladle, thermometer, 5 ml spoon (teaspoon), metal cup or jug, greaseproof paper.

Heat the milk to 68°C (155°F). Cool at once to 32°C (90°F). Add the starter and leave to ripen for 30 minutes if you wish. Add the rennet diluted with 4 × 5 ml spoons (4 teaspoons) tepid water. Stir, reaching down to the bottom of the pan, for three minutes. Cover with a clean cloth and leave to stand for 30 minutes. Test the curd by laying the back of a finger on it. If the curd does not stick to the finger, the curd is ready. (If not ready, leave the curd a little longer.)

Boil the boards and mats (if straw) for 5–10 minutes. Wash plastic moulds and mats in hot water. Place the mats on the boards, then assemble the moulds and place them on one board and mat.

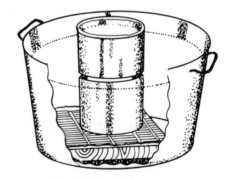

Scald the ladle and a saucer. Scoop a thin slice of curd into the saucer, to finish off the top of the cheese. Ladle the rest of the curd into the mould in thin slices. If there is room at the top of the mould, slip on the saucer slice; if not, slide it on later, when the curd has been inverted.

Keep the room as near 21°C (70°F) as possible. After five to six hours, examine the cheeses. When the curd has shrunk below the top collar of the moulds, remove the top collar, place the second mat on top of the bottom

part of the mould, followed by the board. Carefully, invert the whole mould, boards and mats. Cover with greaseproof paper and leave overnight.

Examine the cheeses. The curd should have shrunk to halfway down the mould and be firm enough to hold its shape when the mould is removed. Remove the mould, sprinkle the cheeses lightly with salt and spread it. Lift the cheeses and brush the undersides with salt. Cover with greaseproof paper

and refrigerate for 12 hours before use.

Note: The curd may take up to 24 hours longer to drain, depending on the weather. For a firmer, more crumbly cheese, leave the cheese to stand at room temperature longer.

Russian Easter Cheese

10 × 100 g (4 oz.) portions

$1\frac{1}{4}$ kg ($2\frac{3}{4}$ lb.) curd cheese
480 ml (1 pt.) sour cream
5 eggs, beaten
100–200 g (4–8 oz.) softened
  unsalted butter
1 × 15 ml spoon (1 tablespoon)
  currants
Grated lemon peel
Vanilla essence
350–480 g (14–16 oz.) sugar
25 g (1 oz.) finely chopped blanched
  and skinned almonds

Equipment: sieve, bowl, 1 × 15 ml
  spoon (tablespoon), fork, saucepan,
  ice, pyramid mould or flowerpot
  (see page 18), muslin, plate,
  weight.

Sieve the cheese into a large bowl and mix in the sour cream, eggs and butter. 100 g (4 oz.) butter will be enough for home-made curd cheese; bought cheese will need more. Turn the mixture into a saucepan and heat to 32°C (90°F), stirring all the time. Do not let the mixture boil. Hold at 32°C (90°F) until the mixture steams, still stirring. When it steams, remove from the heat and place the pan in a bowl of ice. Allow to get quite cold. Add currants, peel, vanilla essence to taste,

27

sugar and almonds. Use 350 g (about 14 oz.) sugar for home-made curd cheese, 480 g (1 lb.) for bought cheese; the mixture should be very sweet, as a good deal of sugar drains out.

Boil the mould or pot and the muslin. Place the mould or pot on a plate and line with a double thickness of muslin which overhangs the edges. Turn in the mixture. Fold the muslin over it and place a light weight on top. Leave overnight in a cool place to drain.

Next day, turn out, cover with a damp cloth and refrigerate until required. Use within five days.

Sage Cheese

Ingredients for Cream Cheese 2, with
  salt and pepper, not sweet
  additions
Equal quantities of fresh, young sage
  leaves and spinach leaves

Equipment: as for Cream Cheese 2.

Make the cheese as described on page 24. Before making, bruise the sage and spinach leaves, squeeze out the juice and add to taste with the rennet.

Varying and Using Soft Cheeses

If you decide to concentrate on soft cheeses, you will probably make at least three or four cheeses at a time. You will find that the curd drains better and keeps a more even texture when processed in quantity; and in any case, it hardly seems worthwhile assembling the equipment, doing the work, and facing the washing-up, just for one small cheese.

Most normal families do not want to eat soft cheeses day after day, without a break. But these cheeses do not keep long, and will probably have lost their first fresh flavour within a few days. They are not long-term preserves like pressed, hard cheeses. So, unless they are eaten at once, you will have to freeze some of them for longer storage, or find other ways to make them last.

This section supplies some ideas. First, it suggests ways in which you can vary soft cheeses to prevent them becoming monotonous when you serve them regularly. Then it suggests ways of using surplus cheeses which will keep them in good condition longer than usual. These should be helpful if you have no home freezer.

You should not attempt to make soft cheeses, however, unless you have a refrigerator to store them in. Even in their longer-lasting forms, they will go sour quite quickly at room temperature. They will still be safe to eat, but their flavour will be unpleasant and you will have to throw them away. Both the milk and your labours as a cheese-maker will be wasted.

Varying Soft Cheeses

The basic ways to vary soft cheeses are listed on page 10 above. By skimming off cream, adding butter, and so on, you can change the consistency of the cheese. You can make a creamy instead of a dry, crumbly curd or the other way round. By leaving the milk to ripen, you can also make an acid curd rather than a bland one. But these changes are not very marked as a rule. Something more is needed to make these cheeses interesting when they appear at meals regularly.

Apart from changing their consistency and sharpness, there are two ways in which to vary soft cheeses: to change what they look like, and what they taste of.

One easy way to change the looks of a soft, unmoulded cheese such as Curd Cheese (page 21) or Crowdie (page 23) is to drain it in a heavily-textured cloth. The cloth leaves the pattern of its weave on the outside of

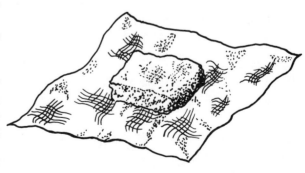

29

the cheese. If you cannot find an interesting textured cloth, pat or press the cheese surface lightly with a pair of Scotch hands. Then impress a pattern on it, just as you do when

'patting up' butter (page 49). Another way, used by the French, is to drain a moulded cheese such as Cambridge cheese on a bed of straw (e.g. a straw mat), or on leaves such as oak or bay leaves. Either leaves a pattern on

the cheese. Sometimes, a cheese is wrapped in the leaves after being drained, so that it appears on the table in a brown 'jacket' instead of as a white or cream-coloured 'bun' or block.

A similar idea is to cover the cheese with toasted dry breadcrumbs, granular (e.g. digestive) biscuit crumbs or

coarse oatmeal. Besides changing its looks, they give it a grainy surface texture which can be attractive, for a change, when it is eaten regularly as 'straight' cheese.

As an alternative to this crumb coating, any slightly acid soft cheese can be sprinkled or coated with coarsley-ground black pepper or other spice berries. A light sprinkling of coarsely-ground juniper berries is intriguing on a creamy cheese. The grains should be scattered on the cheese, then pressed on to its surface lightly. Crushed dried herbs can be used in the same way. Thyme, rosemary or sweet basil all make fragrant coverings. Dill seeds are another alternative.

Besides being used for coating, some spices, herbs and other products can be mixed into a simply-drained soft cheese to make it more interesting. But you must choose the products carefully. Some, such as the spices and herbs above, do a cheese no harm, and may even make it stay fresh a little longer than usual. But other products may make it 'go off' even sooner. Chopped fresh fruit or herbs may carry yeasts which sour the cheese in the yeasts which sour the cheese in the same way as they can infect new curd.

Avoid using, in particular:
- fresh strawberries, raspberries or other soft fruit
- fresh **unpeeled** apples, pears, plums or grapes
- raw unskinned tomatoes or peppers
- dried fruits such as currants or raisins.

You can use safely:
- any peeled or skinned fruit

- well blanched dried fruit
- chopped or flaked skinned nuts.

Here is a short list of some safe 'extras' you can mix into soft cheeses. As a general guide, use one-third to one-half as much extra ingredient as cheese. The exact quantity will depend on the flavour and consistency of the cheese and the other goods. Add, with seasoning, by small spoonfuls until you get the 'mix' you want:

- washed, chopped anchovy fillets, lemon juice
- chopped hard-boiled eggs, softened butter
- chopped chutney
- mixed pickles or piccalilli
- crushed walnuts, chopped raisins or dates
- toasted salted peanuts
- grated onion, curry powder
- chopped gherkin, dill seeds
- mashed canned sardines
- horseradish sauce, melted butter
- finely chopped stuffed olives and walnuts, a little double cream
- chopped canned shrimps or prawns, chopped fresh fennel
- finely chopped cooked chicken, chopped canned pineapple or cooked bacon
- flaked smoked haddock or cod, crumbled hard-boiled egg yolk
- minced cooked ham or bacon, grated spring onion
- chopped pickled onion, melted butter
- chopped candied stem ginger, chopped spring onion, soy sauce
- well seasoned scrambled egg, chopped fresh herbs
- finely chopped chicory, chopped pear, lemon juice
- finely diced cucumber, onion salt

- chopped green or red pimento, garlic salt
- chopped candied stem ginger, honey
- coarsely ground toasted hazelnuts, honey
- chopped crystallised fruits soaked in a little liqueur
- shortbread crumbs, whipped cream (use layered with stewed fruit as a dessert)
- redcurrant jelly
- marmalade, a few drops whisky
- finely chopped mixed peel, a few drops brandy.

These and other salad, fruit or nut 'extras' do not only give a soft cheese a new flavour and interest. They can help to hide the fact that a cheese is slightly too acid, e.g. that it is beginning to go sour. But they will not prevent a cheese getting an acid or 'off' flavour; in other words, they will not make it keep fresh, any more than a coating will. The main point of using them is to vary the cheeses so that they get eaten quickly, before they 'go off'.

Some other products do preserve a cheese for a short time. Vinegar or alcohol (e.g. cider, wine or spirits) stabilise a simply-drained soft cheese if mixed into it. Pickles, chutney, brined olives, gherkins or pickled onions, capers, anchovy fillets and goods like them do so too.

A good way to use these products is this: divide the mass of newly-drained soft cheese into portions likely to be eaten at one meal. Process the ingredients you want to add (e.g. stone and chop olives). Mix each portion of cheese with a different 'extra' ingredient; then spoon or press it into a yoghurt, cream or cottage cheese carton and label it at once. When all the cheese portions are packed and labelled, cover the cartons and stack them in the refrigerator, for use as required.

Using Soft Cheeses

Soft cheeses, well flavoured, can be very useful, not only at table, but for sandwiches in packed meals. But they can still become boring if used too often. So here are some other ways to use these cheeses, so that you do not waste their food value even if they are not wanted for meals just as they are.

The dishes marked ◆ have extra value because the recipes stabilise the cheese. These recipes keep the cheese fresh, with all its goodness, for longer than its natural life.

◆ Soft Cheese Dip or Spread

200 g (8 oz.) any soft cheese
100 g crumbled mature Cheddar or similar cheese
1 × 5 ml spoon (1 teaspoon) French mustard
Finely chopped fresh sage or spring onion to taste
Salt and pepper to taste
Single cream as required or 50 g (2 oz.) melted butter

Sieve the cheeses and pound them together until smooth. Add the mustard, sage or spring onion and seasoning. For a dip, mix in enough single cream to give the consistency you want. For a spread, use melted butter instead, and chill until firm. Store in the refrigerator, well covered, until required.

Sour Cream and Parsley Dip

1 × 100 g (4 fl. oz.) carton soured cream
50 g (2 oz.) sieved curd cheese, yoghurt cheese or crowdie
2 rashers crisply fried bacon
Salt and black pepper to taste
Pinch of curry powder
3 × 5 ml spoons (3 teaspoons) chopped parsley

Combine the cream and soft cheese. Chop the bacon finely and add it with the flavourings and parsley. Add a little milk if a more liquid dip is wanted. Pack in cartons and chill for several hours before use.

◆ Liptauer Cheese Spread

100 g (4 oz.) medium fat soft cheese
100 g (4 oz.) softened slightly salted butter
3 × 5 ml spoons (3 teaspoons) anchovy essence
1 × 10 ml spoon (1 dessertspoon) minced gherkin
1 × 2.5 ml spoon ($\frac{1}{2}$ teaspoon) crushed caraway seeds
1 × 5 ml spoon (1 teaspoon) French mustard
$\frac{1}{2}$ × 2.5 ml spoon ($\frac{1}{4}$ teaspoon) salt
3 × 2.5 ml spoon (1$\frac{1}{2}$ teaspoon) paprika

To decorate (optional):
Capers
Radishes
Black olives

Cream together the cheese and butter until light. Gradually add the other ingredients, and beat lightly until well blended.

To store: put into jars or pots, tapping on the table top two or three times while filling, to knock out any air-bubbles. Cover with a lid or clingfilm, and keep in the refrigerator until required.

To use: mould the cheese into a cone shape, and place on a plate. With the tip of a table knife make ridges lengthways from the top to the base of the cone, forming wavy indentations. Press capers gently into decorative pattern, following the lines of the ridges. Sprinkle a little extra paprika over the cone, and surround it with radishes and black olives.

Variation:

For a richer party spread, use 200 g (8 oz.) cream or full fat soft cheese and 2 × 15 ml spoons (2 tablespoons) butter.

◆ Blue Cheese Spread

Makes 250 g (10 oz.) spread

75 g (3 oz.) any bland soft cheese
75 g (3 oz.) blue cheese
75 g (3 oz.) softened unsalted butter
4 × 10 ml spoons (4 dessertspoons)
    tawny port or cream sherry

Mix the cheeses and butter, and pound or process in an electric blender until smooth. Trickle in the port or sherry until the mixture is almost but not quite saturated. Take care not to add too much, or the mixture will 'weep'. Pack into a jar, tapping on the table top two or three times while filling, to knock out any air-bubbles. Cover with

clingfilm and store in the refrigerator until required.

To use: spread on cocktail snacks or use as a sandwich filling.

◆ Quick Liver Paté

6 × 5 ml spoons (6 teaspoons)
    gelatine
125 ml ($\frac{1}{4}$ pint) hot water
100 g (4 oz.) full fat soft cheese
2 × 15 ml (2 tablespoons) brandy
Salt and pepper to taste
480 g (1 lb.) soft liver sausage

Dissolve the gelatine in the hot water. Cool it. Blend the cheese, brandy, seasoning and liver sausage. Mash together until smooth. Add the dissolved gelatine, and mix well. Turn into a pot or pots, tapping on the table-top two or three times while filling to knock out any air-bubbles. Cover and leave in a cool place or in the refrigerator until set.

To use: serve as a pâté with toast, or use as a sandwich filling or spread.

Cream Cheese and Liver Stuffing

(for chicken, guineafowl or pheasant)

2 shallots
2 × 15 ml spoons (2 tablespoons)
    butter
1 chicken, guineafowl or pheasant
    liver
100 g (4 oz.) lean back bacon
    without rinds
Fresh parsley to taste
75 g (3 oz.) cream cheese
Salt and pepper to taste

Chop the shallots and cook gently in half the butter until soft. Sauté the bird's liver in the remaining butter until tender. Then chop it with the bacon and parsley. Mix in the shallots, cheese and seasoning to taste. Stuff the bird with the mixture.

Soft Cheese Stuffing

(for vegetables, e.g. peppers, tomatoes, or pancakes)

200 g (8 oz.) any soft cheese
1 or 2 eggs (see recipe)
Onion salt to taste
150 g (6 oz.) finely chopped cooked
   meat, fish or second vegetable

Use 2 eggs if the cheese or other filling ingredient is very soft.

Sieve or mash the cheese. Beat in the egg or eggs. Add the seasonings and second ingredient. Taste and adjust the seasoning. Fill into the prepared vegetables or pancakes, place in a greased shallow baking dish and cover loosely with greased foil or vegetable parchment. Bake at 200°C (400°F) Gas 6 until the vegetable or pancake is well heated through, and the filling is set. Peppers or tomatoes will take 25–30 minutes; a pre-baked half marrow will take 35–40 minutes. If using 2 eggs, bake for at least 25 minutes.

Soured cream or natural yoghurt makes a good topping for either the pancakes or vegetables. Put a spoonful on each helping just before serving.

All cheesecakes are best eaten fresh. But most will keep for a few days in the refrigerator, if necessary, if well covered. Baked cheesecakes keep better than gelatine-set ones as a rule. Any fruit or creamy topping should only be added just before serving.

◆ Lemon-Cinnamon Cheesecake

Makes 8 helpings

200 g (8 oz.) digestive biscuits
100 g (4 oz.) butter
50 g (2 oz.) caster sugar
3 × 2.5 ml spoons (1½ teaspoons)
   ground cinnamon
3 eggs, separated
100 g (4 oz.) caster sugar
200 g (8 oz.) curd cheese
100 g (4 oz.) cream cheese
Grated rind and juice of 1 lemon
100 ml (4 fl. oz.) single, double or
   soured cream

Crush the biscuits evenly and finely. Melt the butter gently in a saucepan. Place the crumbs in a bowl, and mix in enough butter to make a crumbly mixture which will stick together when pressed. Keep remaining butter aside. Mix most of the 50 g (2 oz.) sugar and the cinnamon into the crumb mixture. Keep the rest aside. Allow the mixture to cool slightly.

Use the remaining butter to grease the sides and base of an 18–20 cm (7–8 in.) cake tin with a removable base or foil dish which can be cut away from the cheesecake after use. Press most of the crumb mixture evenly over the inside to form a shell. Keep remaining crumb mixture aside.

Mix together the egg yolks and

100 g (4 oz.) sugar, and beat until pale and creamy. Sieve in the cheeses. Mix in lightly the lemon rind and juice, and the cream. Whisk the egg whites to the same consistency as the yolk mixture, and fold in lightly with scooping movements, using a metal spoon; make sure it reaches the bottom of the bowl each time, when turning the mixture over. When well blended in, turn the mixture into the crumb shell, taking care not to lose more air than you can help. Bake at 170°C (325°F) Gas 3 for 50 minutes. Scatter the remaining crumb mixture over the cheesecake, and sprinkle with the remaining sugar and cinnamon. Bake another 15 minutes. Allow to cool in the tin. Slide a knife round the sides to loosen the cake, and turn out on to a serving plate.

This cheesecake stores quite well.

Pear and Gingernut Cheesecake

Makes 8–10 helpings

200 g (8 oz.) gingernuts, crumbled
100 g (4 oz.) butter, melted
100 g (4 oz.) caster sugar
2 eggs, separated
2 × 15 ml spoons (2 tablespoons) gelatine
Juice of 2 lemons and water to make up to 250 ml ($\frac{1}{2}$ pint)
680–700 g (1$\frac{1}{2}$ lb.) bland soft cheese, sieved

2 cooked or canned pears, sieved
2 × 5 ml spoons (2 teaspoons) grated lemon rind
250 ml ($\frac{1}{2}$ pint) double cream, whipped
50–75 g (2–3 oz.) chopped roasted mixed nuts or walnuts

Stir the crumbs into the butter, and press them into the base of a 20–22 cm (8–9 in.) loose-bottomed cake tin. Place 50 g (2 oz.) sugar, the egg yolks, gelatine, lemon juice and water in a heat-proof basin. Stand in a pan of simmering water and stir until the gelatine dissolves. Stir well round the sides of the basin to prevent the egg setting. Remove from the heat, and allow to cool. When almost cold, blend with the cheese, sieved pear, lemon rind and whipped cream. Whisk the egg whites to the same consistency as the main mixture, and fold them in lightly. Spoon the mixture gently on to the crumb base. Chill until set. Remove from the tin and press the nuts on to the sides of the cheesecake.

Quick Orange and Yoghurt Cheesecake

Makes 4–6 helpings

200 g (8 oz.) almond macaroons
75 g (3 oz.) butter, melted
200 g (8 oz.) low fat curd cheese
125 ml ($\frac{1}{4}$ pint) natural yoghurt
2 × 15 ml spoons (2 tablespoons) liquid honey
Grated rind of 1 orange
5 crystallised or candied orange slices

Crush the macaroons between two

sheets of paper, using a rolling pin. Make fine even crumbs. Stir them into the melted butter and press firmly into a lined and lightly greased 16–17 cm (6½–7 in.) sandwich tin. Either chill until firm in the refrigerator, or bake 'blind' for 10 minutes at 180°C (350°F) Gas 4, then chill.

Sieve the cheese and mix with the yoghurt, honey and orange rind. Spoon into the pie shell. Refrigerate for 2–3 hours before use. Decorate with the crystallised or candied orange slices just before serving.

Blackcurrant Cheesecake

Makes 4–6 helpings

25 g (1 oz.) butter
1 × 15 ml spoon (1 tablespoon) golden syrup
125 g (5 oz.) digestive biscuits, crushed
250 ml (½ pint) skim milk or dried milk powder made up with water
3 eggs, separated
50 g (2 oz.) caster sugar
1 pkt. (½ oz.) gelatine
200 g (8 oz.) cream cheese, softened
1 × 2.5 ml spoon (½ teaspoon) grated lemon rind
1 × 15 ml spoon (1 tablespoon) lemon juice
200 g (8 oz.) prepared blackcurrants
4 × 15 ml spoons (4 tablespoons) water
2 × 5 ml spoons (2 teaspoons) arrowroot

Grease and line a 15 cm (6 in.) square or an 18 cm (7 in.) round cake tin with a removable base. Melt the butter and syrup gently in a saucepan. Stir in the biscuit crumbs. Press the mixture into the cake tin, and leave in cool place until firm.

Heat the skim milk and egg yolks in a saucepan, stirring continuously. When the mixture thickens, remove from the heat, stir in the 25 g (1 oz.) sugar and leave to cool. Soften the gelatine in 2 × 15 ml spoons (2 tablespoons) water in a heatproof basin. While it softens, whisk the egg whites until stiff. Stand the basin containing the gelatine in simmering water, and stir until the gelatine dissolves. Add gradually to the softened cheese with the skim milk custard and the lemon juice and rind. Whisk the mixture until it begins to thicken; then fold in the whisked egg whites lightly, and spoon the mixture into the prepared tin. Leave to set.

Place the blackcurrants in a saucepan with the water and sugar. Bring gently to the boil, and cook for two minutes. Remove from the heat, and drain off the juice into a saucepan. Blend 2 × 5 ml spoons (2 teaspoons) juice with the arrowroot. Add to the main mixture in the pan, and bring gently to the boil, stirring continuously. Add the fruit. Cool, but do not allow to set.

Remove the base of the tin, and peel the paper off. Place the cheesecake on a cake board or rack placed over a dish. Pour the blackcurrant sauce over it. Serve at once.

Belgian Cheese Flan

Makes 4–6 helpings

175–200 g (7½–8 oz.) puff pastry, home-made or frozen

200 g (8 oz.) full fat curd cheese
2 eggs, beaten
125 ml ($\frac{1}{4}$ pint) double cream
Grated rind and juice of $\frac{1}{2}$ lemon
35 g (1$\frac{1}{2}$ oz.) caster sugar

Roll out the pastry thinly on a floured surface and line a 20 cm (8 in.) flan ring with it. Prick the base well. Chill for 30 minutes. Line with vegetable parchment and baking beans, and bake 'blind' at 220°C (425°F) Gas 7 for 15 minutes. Remove the beans and lining parchment, and bake for a further five minutes.

Mix the eggs into the cheese one by one, and heat until smoothly blended. Stir in the cream, lemon rind and juice, and sugar; do not beat. Reduce the oven heat to 180°C (350°F) Gas 4. Turn the cheese mixture into the flan ring, and return to the oven for 25 minutes or until the filling is set. Leave to get quite cold before serving.

Austrian Economy Cheese Flan

Makes 4–5 helpings

100 g (4 oz.) rusks, crushed
35 g (1$\frac{1}{2}$ oz.) margarine, melted
200 g (8 oz.) cream or full fat curd
    cheese
25 g caster sugar
1 standard egg yolk
60 ml ($\frac{1}{8}$ pint) double cream
Grated rind of $\frac{1}{2}$ orange or lemon
12 g ($\frac{1}{2}$ oz.) sultanas (optional)
1 standard egg white, whisked until
    stiff
$\frac{1}{2}$ orange and $\frac{1}{2}$ lemon thinly sliced for
    decoration

Mix together the rusk crumbs and margarine and press into a 15 cm (6 in.) flan ring or pie plate, to cover the base and sides. Mix together all the remaining ingredients except the egg white and decorative fruit slices. Fold in the whisked egg white. Turn into the crumb shell, and bake at 190°C (375°F) Gas 5, for 40–45 minutes or until the filling is set. Cool. Decorate with alternate slices of orange and lemon round the edge of the flan.

Chocolate and Yoghurt Cheesecake

Makes 6–8 helpings

For the pastry:
100 g (4 oz.) plain flour
Pinch of salt
50 g (2 oz.) butter
25 g (1 oz.) caster sugar
1 egg yolk
3 × 2.5 ml spoons (1$\frac{1}{2}$ teaspoons)
    water

For the filling:
2 eggs, separated
75 g (3 oz.) caster sugar
200 g (8 oz.) soft cheese
2 × 15 ml spoons (2 tablespoons)
    single cream
Grated rind and juice of 1 lemon
50 g (2 oz.) flour
50 g (2 oz.) sultanas
75 g (3 oz.) plain chocolate
1 egg white

For the topping:
125 ml ($\frac{1}{4}$ pint) yoghurt
25 g (1 oz.) icing sugar
75 g (3 oz.) coating chocolate

Make the pastry first. Sift the flour and salt into a basin, and rub in the butter until the mixture resembles fine bread-crumbs. Stir in the sugar. Mix the egg yolk into the water, blend well, and add to the dry ingredients. Mix well, to form a firm dough. Chill for one hour, then roll out on a floured surface, into a 20 cm (8 in.) circle. Grease a 20 cm (8 in.) loose bottomed cake tin, and press the pastry circle into the base gently. Chill.

Make the filling by whisking the egg yolks and sugar together until light and thick. Blend together the cheese, cream, grated rind and juice and the flour, smoothing out any lumps. Blend with the egg-sugar mixture lightly, then fold in the sultanas. Melt the chocolate on a plate over simmering water, and stir it into the main mixture.

Whisk the egg white until stiff and fold in gently. Turn into the prepared pastry case, and bake at 190°C (375°F) Gas 5 for $\frac{3}{4}$–1 hour, or until the filling is firm.

Combine the yoghurt and icing sugar, spoon over the cheesecake. Raise the oven heat to 220°C (425°F) Gas 7 and return the cheesecake to the over for 5–10 minutes until set. Allow the cheesecake to cool completely. Melt the covering chocolate. Lay a sheet of foil on a marble slab or other cool surface. Spread the chocolate on it with a palette knife. When almost set, divide into 2.5 cm (1 in.) squares using a ruler and a knife point. Allow to set firmly. Peel off the foil. Arrange the chocolate squares in an overlapping circle round the cheesecake.

Making Hard Cheeses

Making hard cheeses at home is not difficult although it involves more work and takes longer than making the simply-drained soft cheeses.

The Smallholder's Cheese already mentioned (page 15) is the most

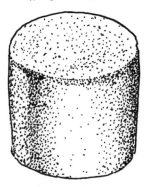

practical one for the cheese-maker on a small scale to tackle. The quantity of milk needed is easy to handle and any fair-sized domestic pans can be used. The cheeses do not take up much space and need not be stored for long. They are a practical size for an average family to use; and if, by ill chance, they spoil, only a few gallons of milk will have been wasted.

Once you know how to make this Smallholder's Cheese, you will know, in principle, how to make any hard or semi-hard cheese. So, if you progress from a smallholding to a farm, or find that you can get milk in bulk, you can then try making cheeses on a larger scale with the benefit of some knowledge. There are plenty of recipes for Cheddar, Cheshire and Wensleydale-style cheeses. The books marked * in the reading list on page 72 contain examples of them.

Make sure that you have adequate facilities before tackling these larger cheeses. As mentioned above, to make the English cheeses successfully, they should be at least the sizes given in the Table on page 7 and this means using a lot of milk, very large pans and some special heavy equipment. These cheeses take a long time to mature and their care and handling involves some heavy work.

Equipment

The list of equipment needed for making Smallholder's Cheese may look long at first glance. But you will have most of the items already, either for making soft cheeses or for general kitchen use.
You will need:
- a large pan
- a lid or cloth to cover it
- a dairy thermometer
- a ladle
- 5 ml spoons (teaspoons)
- wooden spoons for stirring
- jugs
- a palette knife
- a curd knife
- close-textured cotton cloth
- a tray
- two to three squares muslin
- Smallholder cheese mould and follower
- weights or a press

muslin bandages
lard, or cornflour paste.

All these items must be boilable, so that they can be sterilised. Take care to sterilise them properly before you begin a cheese-making session, and keep them sterile. Remember that the air is full of bacteria, so turn jugs and basins upside down or cover them with sterile cloths if you do not use them straight away. Put spoons and knives into a sterile jug or bowl and cover them with a sterile cloth too. Turn the tray upside down. Cover the mould. (Boil muslin cloths to be used in the cheese-making just before you need them.)

The Smallholder's Cheese mould or 'chessit' looks like two sections of ordinary drain-pipe; do not, however, use ordinary drain-pipe sections for moulds. The material they are made of is not purified to the standard needed for cheese-making.

Ingredients

By comparison with the list of equipment, the ingredients for the cheese are modest. You will need:

15 litres (3 gallons) whole milk or part whole and part skimmed milk
125 ml ($\frac{1}{4}$ pt.) starter
1 × 5 ml spoon (1 teaspoon) cheese rennet
25 g (1 oz.) salt

Now, here are the directions for making your cheese. Note that they are given under headings. These are terms used by all cheese-makers, professional and amateur, to describe the processes they use in making any cheese.

Heat Treatment

Heat the milk to 68°C (155°F). Cool it at once to 32°C (90°F).

Startering and Ripening

Add the 125 ml ($\frac{1}{4}$ pt.) starter and stir it in well. Leave to ripen for 30 minutes.

Renneting

Place 1 × 5 ml spoon (1 teaspoon) cheese rennet in a sterilised jug. Add 20 ml (4 teaspoons) tepid water. Mix well. Pour the mixture into the milk. Stir in thoroughly. Leave for 30–40 minutes. If using whole milk, flick the top of the milk with a spoon during the first five minutes of setting

to prevent a cream layer forming during setting. After 30 minutes, test whether the curd is firm enough by laying the back of a finger on the milk surface. If no milk sticks to it, the curd is ready.

Cutting the Curd

Using a palette knife, cut the curd into 1 cm ($\frac{1}{2}$ in.) strips. Then cut at right angles to these strips to form 1 cm ($\frac{1}{2}$ in.) columns of curd. Next, using a curd knife, make horizontal cuts through

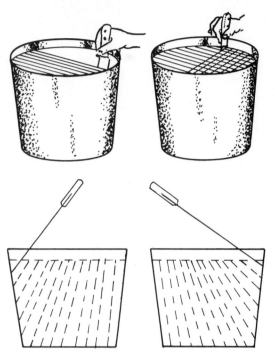

the body of the curd so that cubes of curd are formed, each about 1 cm ($\frac{1}{2}$ in.) deep. Slide the palette knife round the outside edge of the curd, to loosen it from the pan. Leave to stand for 5–10 minutes until some whey has formed on top.

Scalding

Place the pan over very gentle heat. During the next 30 minutes, gradually raise the temperature of the curd to 38°C (100°F). Throughout this 30 minutes, stir the curds and whey gently with the hand. On no account let the temperature of the mixture rise above

38°C (100°F). When the 30 minutes is up, remove the pan from the heat and stir for a further five minutes.

Pitching

Leave the curd for 30 minutes, to let it settle on the bottom of the pan.

Running the Whey

Ladle off most of the whey. Tip the rest of the curds and whey into a sterilised cloth and form the cloth into a bundle by winding one corner round the other three. Place the bundle on a tray, tilted to let the whey run off.

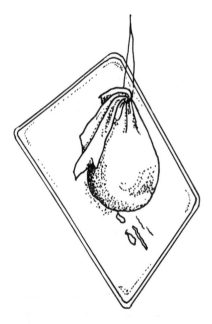

After 15 minutes, untie the bundle. Cut the curd into four long slices. Pile them one on another. Re-tie the cloth, tightening it a little. Repeat this process three times at 15 minute intervals, re-stacking the curd slices each time. If you wish, cut the curd slices in half and turn them over so that the edges lie in the centre.

Milling and Salting

When the curd is quite firm, break it up into small pieces the size of a cherry. Sprinkle with 25 g (1 oz.) salt. Toss the curd, to mix in the salt.

Moulding

Boil a square of muslin for 10 minutes. Line the cheese mould with this and stand the mould on a tray. Press the

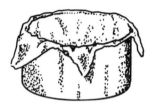

curd into the mould, packing it down thoroughly. Cover with a corner of the muslin and place the wooden follower on top to act as a base for a weight.

Pressing

Place a 3 kg (about 7 lb.) weight on top of the follower and leave for two hours. Then increase the weight to about 12 kg (about 28 lb.) and leave overnight.

Second Day: Remove the cheese, in its muslin from the mould. If it has no cracks in it, dip it into a sink of hot (66°C, 150°F) water (*bathing*) for about 20 seconds. Wrap it in a fresh square of newly boiled muslin and replace it upside down in the mould. Pull up the muslin to prevent creases forming in the cheese. Double the pressure on the cheese.

Third Day: Repeat the process above, omitting the bathing. Remember to turn the cheese upside down again when turning it. Double the pressure on it again. By the end of this day, the cheese should be firm enough to be removed from the mould. If it is not, leave it in the mould for a further 48 hours.

Bandaging and Ripening

Cut a piece of muslin as wide as the cheese is deep and one and a half times its circumference in length. Cut two pieces of muslin to act as caps for each

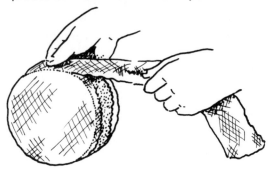

end (four in all). Using lard or cornflour paste, stick the caps on each end. Wrap the long bandage firmly round the cheese, sticking it down as you do so.

Curing

Store the cheese on an open-rack shelf at a temperature of 10–16°C (50–60°F). Turn the cheese upside down every day for 10–14 days.

Looking After Your Cheeses

If you cure your cheeses carefully, they will be ready to eat in three to four weeks, although their flavour will improve if you keep them longer. But they need a little more care than just being turned upside down daily for a fortnight.

First, make sure that the temperature of your storage place is right—somewhere between 10° and 16°C (50°–60°F). It should be airy and without draughts. Make sure, too, that the shelves on which you store your cheeses are clean and dry. They must not have been scrubbed with detergent, but should have been washed with very hot water and allowed to dry completely.

Next, label your cheeses, in particular with the date when they should be ready for eating. This date is surprisingly easy to forget; probably because the cheeses need to mature for at least a fortnight after you stop turning them and during this time you will most likely leave them alone. If you rely just on memory, you may well try to eat one too soon while it still tastes raw and its texture is 'gummy'; or you may leave a batch in storage too long because you do not want to take a chance on its being ready. Another easy mistake to make is to stack a stray unlabelled cheese from an old batch among new ones so that it ripens for twice as long as usual. This is not always a bad thing. But if the cheese is left on the shelf until most of the new batch have been used, it may be dry and too strong by the time you eat it.

You should not, in fact, leave your cheeses entirely alone after you finish turning them. Check the temperature of your storage place every other day or when there is any marked weather change. You should, if possible, have fly screens on your windows; but if you have not, chase out any flies. Do not spray them. Inspect the cheeses too. If they show any signs of mould, brush it off with a clean brush and brush the surrounding shelf as well. It may be a good idea to brush or rub the cheeses with lard or to dip them in wax after a week.

Given this care, your cheeses should mature evenly and well and give you many pleasant meals.

Butter Making

Butter is a natural food to use with cheese eaten 'straight', or when it is used for cooking. 'Bread and cheese' usually means to us bread-and-butter with cheese. Grated cheese used for crusty toppings melts better and more evenly when mixed with butter. Toasted cheese needs a scraping of butter spread on the cheese flakes before being cooked.

Besides this, several of our soft cheeses and thick yoghurt too, are usually made with skimmed milk. So if you are a cheese-maker, the cream from the milk can be used for butter-making and the skim milk for cheese, making use of all the milk, and giving you two products instead of one.

If only some members of a family want low-fat, skim-milk cheese for health reasons or slimming, butter 'fills in' for the rest the nourishment which the cheeses lack. Here are the food values of 25 g (1 oz.) butter:

- calories   211
- protein   0.1 g
- fat   23.4 g
- calcium   4 mg
- iron   Trace
- vitamin A   850 IU
- vitamin D   17 IU

As you can see from this, butter contains a very large amount of fat. In fact, butter is just preserved pure cream, condensed and solid because most of its fluid and the substances dissolved in it have been separated from the fat by churning.

Because it is packed solid, it takes a lot of cream to make even a small pat of butter. On average, you need the cream from 10–15 litres (2½–3 gallons)

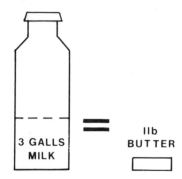

of milk to make 450 g (1 lb.) butter. So, if you have to buy your milk or cream at a commercial rate, you should calculate very carefully whether it is worth your while making your own butter.

However, if you have your own cow or goat, or access to a good supply of cheap milk, it may well be profitable to make your own butter, especially if your family eats home-made cheese. You will not only have a ready-to-hand use for the skim milk and buttermilk but also you can use the same premises and equipment for butter-making as for making cheese, except for maybe buying a separator and churn (page 45 below). So you will not have much capital outlay, or much to spend on ingredients.

Before you begin butter-making, make sure that you have both the right conditions and the tools just as in cheese-making (pages 16–17). If possible, you should make it in a different room from your kitchen, to prevent it being contaminated by harmful bacteria. For butter-making on a large scale, you should really have three rooms, as you should for cheese-making; one where you ripen the cream, one where you make the butter, and a scullery where you sterilise your equipment. But this is not necessary if you only make butter for home use. You can manage quite well in a single room, provided you can keep it at an even temperature between 10° and 16°C (50° and 60°F), and it has a stove, adequate electric plugs (e.g. for a steriliser and electric mixer) and a sink with hot and cold water.

Equipment

The equipment you need will depend on the scale of your butter-making operations. For small-scale butter-making, using as much ordinary kitchen equipment as possible, you will only need:

- a hair or nylon strainer or sieve
- shallow setting pans
- crocks in which to ripen cream
- various sizes of boilable bowls for cream, skim milk etc.
- an electric mixer and bowl
- butter-muslin
- a wooden chopping or pastry board
- Scotch hands
- a palette knife or spatula
- a dairy thermometer
- dry salt
- a set of scales
- vegetable parchment or clingfilm
- refrigerator space.

If you can afford special equipment

(essential for larger-scale butter-making), invest in:

- a steriliser
- a separator
- a churn
- a butter worker
- a butter scoop
- milk and cream pails
- an acidimeter (which tells you how much acid the cream has).

Just as in cheese-making, both your equipment and your milk must be completely clean. Sterilise your equipment in the same way as for cheese-making (page 18) before you use it. Give it time to cool before use. Clean the milk if necessary by straining it before beginning the cream separation and butter-making.

It is perfectly possible to separate the cream from the rest of the milk in the traditional way, i.e. by letting the milk stand in shallow pans until the cream has risen, then skimming it off the surface. But it is wasteful because a certain amount of cream gets re-mixed with the rest of the milk and is left behind.

So, if you possibly can, invest in a separator. Small domestic models are quite easy to get from stockists of

dairying equipment. They vary, but most work on the same principle. One common type consists of a number of metal cones which fit on to a spindle (one on top of another, like a stack of clown's hats) and spin round with it when the machine is switched on. The milk is fed into the machine from a large pan; and as it swirls round and round, between the spinning metal cones, the movement's force throws the thin, lightweight milk outwards against the sides of the cones and it flows out through a pipe into a churn or pail. At the same time, the heavier, fat-rich cream is sucked into a smaller pipe in the centre and runs out into a small bowl. It trickles out gently. But the spinning motion of the cones makes the skim milk bubbly, with a mass of froth on top. So always have a container to receive it which holds one-and-a-half times as much milk as you are putting through the separator. It will save a messy overflow on the floor. (In Scotland, the froth is called Butter-bells and is used as a drink.)

A separator takes off all the cream, so it saves both waste and work. It has other advantages too. These are:

- the milk is fresh and sweet because it need not stand for the cream to rise
- one need not have space for the setting pans in the dairy
- it is less work to take the milk straight to the separator
- the cream is fresh and sweet, and so it is easy to thin down and to ripen with a starter.

Once you have cream, you can begin your butter-making proper. There are two kinds which you can make. One is 'Sweet Cream' butter made from fresh cream; it is mildly flavoured, with a firm, waxy, smooth texture, good for making pastry and biscuits. The other is 'Lactic' butter, which is full-flavoured, soft and fine in texture, so that it 'creams' easily and is good for cake-making and home sweet-making. It is made from cream which has been 'ripened' or matured, either naturally or with the help of a 'starter'.

Lactic butter is popular because of its full nutty flavour and its softness for spreading. But it is not as easy to make or keep, especially on a small scale, as sweet cream butter. One must either have a regular daily supply of cream for natural ripening, or one must care for a starter culture in the same way as a cheese starter culture (page 19 above); and for both methods,

one needs a ripening room with a constant temperature of 15°–16°C (58°–60°F), where the cream can stand. Lactic butter is easy to churn. But after churning, the butter's soft texture may make it difficult for a beginner to work or 'pat up'; and the completed butter must be used or disposed of fairly quickly, since it matures with keeping and may only be at its best in about six weeks, less good afterwards.

If, however, one wants to make butter on a fairly large scale, or for sale, and one has the space and the equipment (e.g. an 'end-over-end' churn), lactic butter is more economical to make than sweet cream butter because one loses less fat in the churn. The usual way to ripen the cream naturally is to mix together the cream of two or three days milkings, stirring each new supply into the previously accumulated cream thoroughly, to make sure it ripens evenly all through. The cream should be stirred several times each

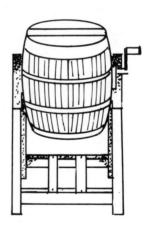

day. When it has a clean acid taste (i.e. it contains about 0.5% lactic acid), it is left to stand for about 12 hours without adding more cream and is then churned. Usually, it must be churned twice a week in summer, but in winter once a week will probably do. Using a starter does not give you less work; but the butter is likely to keep better because harmful bacteria are not given time to attack the cream while it ripens and because it is heat-treated (pasteurised).

The starter is used in much the same way as a cheese starter. It can be bought from most agricultural colleges and dairy schools, and instructions about the proportion to add are given with it. To use it, a small quantity of freshly separated cream is heated to 66°C (150°F), then cooled at once to about 21°C (70°F) in summer, 24°C (75°F) in winter. The starter culture is added as the makers direct and is well stirred in; and the cream is allowed to stand for about 24 hours, in a clean, well-ventilated room with a temperature of about 16°C (60°F). By that time, it should be well thickened and some of it is used to innoculate another small quantity of cream, also heat-treated. After yet another 24 hours, the starter is ready to use for making butter out of a third, larger lot of cream, heat-treated like the first two. The starter cream should be renewed every day in summer, about three times a week in winter; if it begins to taste bitter, it should be thrown away and a new bottle of culture bought.

Using a starter is the safest method of butter-making because you can control what happens at every stage; this is important for anyone who wants to make butter for sale. (One must also comply with government requirements for the quality of the butter, e.g. its fat and moisture content.) But it is a lot of work if one just wants to make butter to use at home and it means making butter regularly, without a break. So the preparation method given below is for the simpler sweet cream butter, which you can make when it suits you, with either dairy equipment or just using kitchen tools. Sweet cream butter has other advantages too. Its firmness makes it easy to work and to 'pat up', and makes it excellent for sealing potted meats and cheeses.

Having scalded or scrubbed all your equipment to sterilise it, it is wise to heat-treat the cream as well, to reduce the risk of it 'going off' quickly. Heat it to 77°C (170°F), then cool it quickly and store it in the refrigerator overnight.

Next day, check how thick the cream is. If it has set or is as thick as double cream, thin it down with cold or tepid water (see below), until if you run a little cream over a wooden spoon, most of it will drip off and the wood's grain will just be visible. It should still be thicker than single cream, however.

Next, check its temperature. If it is too cold, it will take a very long time to churn. If it is too warm, it will churn quickly but the butter grains will be large and soft and the butter will be sticky. It should be at a temperature between 14°C (56°F) on a warm day and 17°C (62°F) on a cold day. Use tepid water to thin the cream, to get it to the right temperature. Make sure that all your tools are cold.

For churning any butter, you can either invest in an end-over-end churn like the one in the illustration on page 47, or in a small glass churn like the one in the centre of the cover picture. But if you do not want to go to this expense, at least at first, you can make the butter with an ordinary kitchen electric mixer. If you buy a churn, the manufacturer supplies full instructions for use with it, so the electric-mixer method is the one given here.

To Make Butter with an Electric Mixer

Half-fill the mixer bowl with cream at the right temperature. Start whisking it at the lowest speed and continue whisking gently until the cream begins to thicken. Then you can add more cream gradually, still whisking. You can increase the speed while the added cream is still liquid, but as soon as it begins to thicken, reduce the speed again. Continue whisking until the mixture begins to separate and its colour changes to yellow. Tiny grains of butter will appear in it, which look like scrambled egg.

When the whole mixture looks like scrambled egg, stop the mixer. Mix the butter grains with a spatula until they are slightly larger and a little clear

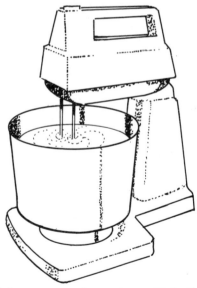

liquid separates from them. This is the buttermilk. Drain it off and continue working the butter until the grains begin to stick together. The grains will

separate from the buttermilk best if they are small, so do not try to make them a solid mass. Drain the buttermilk off again if required.

Now test the temperature of the butter with a dairy thermometer, and • add what is called 'breaking' water at a temperature 2° lower than the temperature of the butter. Add enough water to float the grains. Strain it off and repeat the same process twice, each time using water 2° cooler than the time before. You do this to wash out the buttermilk with dissolved milk sugar or lactose in it. If you do not do it, the butter will be soggy and turn sour very quickly.

After straining the water off for the third time, tip the butter into a sieve or a muslin bag and let it drain for a few minutes. Then tip the butter on to a wooden board. Sprinkle it with about 1 × 5 ml spoon (1 teaspoon) of salt for each 450 g (1 lb.) butter grains. Press and squeeze the grains together, either with Scotch hands, or using your own hands or a spatula. Prop up one end of the board so that any moisture runs off and squeeze the butter grains to get rid of as much moisture as possible. This process is called 'working' the butter.

Work the butter until you have worked in the salt evenly and have squeezed out as much buttermilk as you can. Then pat the butter out fairly flat. Fold it over and squeeze it into a block shape with Scotch hands. Weigh it and divide it into pieces and size and weight you want. Form them into neat blocks or round pats and decorate them with ridged lines or some other pattern, with the Scotch hands. Wrap the blocks or pats in greaseproof paper and store them in the refrigerator.

Using Whey and Buttermilk

When you make cheese or butter, you are left with a lot of whey or buttermilk. In the past, these were always used for drinks or for cooking, and were very popular. But most people find them difficult to get now, so the ways of using them have been forgotten. It is a pity because it is wasteful to throw them away. They are nourishing, especially for children, since they contain quite a lot of the goodness of milk, such as the milk sugar or lactose.

Buttermilk is richer than whey. It has lost little more than the whole milk's fat and Vitamin A. Thus it is very similar to skim milk and can be used for most things that skim milk is used for. There are also special uses.

Whey is thinner because the curds from which it has drained have picked up a good many more of the substances originally dissolved in the whole milk (page 10). But this does not mean that it has no food value left. It is certainly worth using.

Whey is used mostly for making tangy drinks and for whey butter. Bread slices soaked in whey and then toasted and served well buttered are delicious; and it is, of course, an ingredient of the traditional curds and whey which Miss Muffet ate, and which still make a good children's dessert. Recipes for all these are given on pages 51–53. Whey also makes a good substitute for fish stock, both in sauces and for poaching fish. Set with gelatine, it makes a light, delicately-flavoured aspic.

Buttermilk can also be used for refreshing drinks, including milk shakes. It makes interesting dips, dressings, soups, jellies and baked goods. In the past, one of its most important uses was to make curds for cheesecakes and other desserts, and for crowdie, curd and 'pot' cheeses; and you can use buttermilk to make curds for these now, if you like the texture and flavour of buttermilk curd. When drained, it is dryish compared with the curd made by a cheese or yoghurt starter (page 19), by essence of rennet or cheese rennet (page 21). It also has a slightly acid flavour, even when the curd is made from fresh milk.

It is important to remember, if you use home-produced buttermilk, that its flavour will vary, depending on whether you have used fresh or ripened cream to make your butter. If you have made lactic butter from ripened cream, the buttermilk will have a sharper flavour and will be more suited to making dips, dressings and curds for savoury dishes than to making dessert, cakes or sweet scones. Sweet cream butter yields a milder-flavoured buttermilk which is better for sweet dishes.

People who do not make butter at home can sometimes get commercially-made buttermilk, generally at health food stores. It is usually labelled 'cultured buttermilk' and this means that special starter has been used. Its flavour is mild compared with buttermilk obtained by making lactic butter from naturally ripened cream, but is sharper than buttermilk from sweet cream butter. Its consistency is different too. It is smooth and velvety, like cream, and often so thick that it has to be scraped out of its carton.

Another difference to remember is that cultured buttermilk lacks the flavour and scent of local pasture found in the milk of a single cow or a small herd. So, if you use cultured buttermilk for a recipe from an old book, do not expect the result to taste just as it did in the past. Drinks, especially, will not have the same scent or flavour from meadow grass or perhaps clover, although they will have a richer, smoother texture.

Remember these points, too, if you use cultured buttermilk for one of the recipes below. They are designed, like the old ones, for using buttermilk from home-made (sweet cream) butter. So the flavourings may need adapting slightly.

Green Whey

200 ml (8 fl. oz.) whey
Juice of $\frac{1}{2}$ lemon, or to taste
Pinch of salt
1 × 5 ml spoon (1 teaspoon) sugar

Taste the whey. Strain in only enough lemon juice to give it slight sharpness; it should hardly be noticeable. Add the other flavourings just as cautiously. They should only underline the whey's natural flavour, not dominate it. Chill very thoroughly before serving. Makes a refreshing drink for a hot afternoon.

Whey Butter

Whey from cheese-making
Boiling water
Starter
Salt

Let the whey from cheese-making stand undisturbed for 24 hours, then skim off any cream which has risen to the top. Put the cream in a heatproof container and add about four times its volume of boiling water, to clarify the fat and get rid of any cheesy flavour. Leave for 24 hours, then skim off the cream and put it into the basin or pail in which cream is collected for churning. Add the same amount of starter as for ordinary lactic butter.

Every day, treat fresh whey in the same way, adding its cream when clarified to the cream already collected. Stir the old and new cream together thoroughly. If the cream sours quickly, add a little salt. Churn like ordinary butter, taking care to wash thoroughly with the 'breaking' water.

Whey Toast

For each helping use:
1 large square slice white bread
    without crusts
50 ml (2 fl. oz.) whey
Butter as required

Dip the bread in the whey; it must be moist all through, but not soggy. Toast on both sides to the degree of brownness you prefer. Spread generously with butter. Use as a 'bed' for toasted cheese and similar dishes, or serve hot with jam.

Curds and Whey

500 ml (1 pint) milk
2 × 15 ml spoons (2 tablespoons)
    lemon juice
Sugar to taste
Ground cinnamon or grated nutmeg
    to taste
Chilled single cream

Heat the milk to 38°C (100°F). Pour it into a heatproof basin or jug and strain in the lemon juice. Leave to stand for 1–2 hours until a firm curd forms. If the curd remains loose and soft, stand the container in simmering water until the curd draws together and becomes solid. Cool thoroughly. Drain off the whey, and sweeten and flavour it to taste. Sprinkle sugar on the curds. Serve the curds well chilled, with single cream poured over them and with the sweetened whey as a sauce.

Buttermilk Curds and Whey

Makes 4 helpings

250 ml ($\frac{1}{2}$ pint) rich fresh milk
500 ml (1 pint) chilled fresh
    buttermilk
Caster sugar to taste
Single cream
Pinch of salt
Vanilla essence or ground cinnamon
    to taste

Make the milk scalding (not boiling) hot, and quickly stir in the buttermilk. Leave to stand until a firm curd forms. If the curd remains loose and soft, reheat it until it draws together and becomes solid. Cool thoroughly. Then tip the curd into a thin cloth laid on a sieve placed over a basin. Allow to drain until set and crumbly.

Turn gently out of the cloth on to a board, and pat square with Scotch hands or a palette knife. Cut into square individual servings, and lift them into four serving bowls. Sprinkle each with caster sugar and chill. When ready to use, pour over each a small quantity of single cream flavoured with sifted icing sugar, a pinch of salt, and vanilla essence or cinnamon to taste. Flavour some of the whey like the cream and serve it in a jug as a sauce.

Cheese and Buttermilk Dip

(an electric blender recipe)

3–6 × 15 ml spoons (3–6
    tablespoons) buttermilk
4 drops Tabasco sauce
1 small carrot, chopped
$\frac{1}{2}$ onion, chopped
3 sprigs parsley without stalks
$\frac{1}{2}$ clove garlic, peeled
250–300 g (10–12 oz.) curd cheese
    (page 21)
Salt and freshly-ground black pepper
    to taste

Put 3 × 15 ml spoons (3 tablespoons) buttermilk and all the other ingredients except the seasoning into the goblet of the blender in the order given, while running the machine at speed 2. (If the blender is a small one, process half the ingredients first, then repeat the process.) Blend until the solid ingredients are very finely chopped. Stop the machine and scrape down if required. Remove the mixture from the goblet, taste and season as desired. Add the extra buttermilk if a thinner dip or dressing is wanted. Chill before use.

Buttermilk Puffs

Makes about 24 puffs

200 g (8 oz.) buttermilk curds made as in 'Buttermilk Curds and Whey'
3 eggs
1 egg white
1 × 2.5 ml spoon ($\frac{1}{2}$ teaspoon) each salt, grated nutmeg and ground cinnamon
150–200 g (6–8 oz.) soft white breadcrumbs as required

Tip the drained curd into a basin. Beat the eggs and egg white into the curd until well blended and smooth. Add the spices, and enough breadcrumbs to make a paste which will stand in peaks. Lay greased paper or vegetable parchment on a flat baking sheet, and heat the oven to 170°C (325°F) Gas 3. Shape large teaspoonfuls of the mixture into small meringue-shaped balls on the paper. Bake in the centre of the oven for 20–30 minutes or until firm and beginning to brown. Eat with fish or cheese dishes instead of potatoes or dumplings. Alternatively, sweeten the mixture before baking with 1–2 × 5 ml spoons (1–2 teaspoons) caster sugar, and use as a 'nibbler' with mid-morning coffee.

Blackthorn Buttermilk Cake

200 g (8 oz.) currants
125 ml ($\frac{1}{4}$ pint) still cider
480 g (1 lb.) plain flour
100 g (4 oz.) unsalted butter
1 × 5 ml spoon (1 teaspoon) grated nutmeg
2 × 5 ml spoons (2 teaspoons) cream of tartar
1 × 5 ml spoon (1 teaspoon) bicarbonate of soda
200 g (8 oz.) caster sugar
2 eggs, beaten
125 ml ($\frac{1}{4}$ pint) buttermilk
2 × 5 ml spoons (2 teaspoons) lemon juice

Steep the currants in the cider until well plumped. Sift the flour and rub in the butter until the mixture resembles fine crumbs. Sift together the nutmeg, cream of tartar, soda and sugar, and add to the mixture. Stir in. Mix the eggs into the buttermilk with the lemon juice. Mix the cider and currants and the buttermilk mixture, into the dry goods alternately adding about one-third each time. Mix well to blend. Place the mixture in a 20 cm (8 in.) square cake tin, well greased or lined with vegetable parchment. Bake at 170°C (325°F) Gas 3 for about two hours, or until the cake is springy and brown. Cool well before cutting.

Rich Iced Coffee

Makes 1–2 drinks

2 × 5 ml spoons (2 teaspoons) instant coffee powder
Sugar to taste
250 ml ($\frac{1}{2}$ pint) buttermilk

Mix the instant coffee powder with just enough boiling water to make it liquid. Sweeten it to suit your usual taste. Cool. When cold, mix with the buttermilk. Stir thoroughly to blend. Chill. Serve very cold in long glasses.

Making Yoghurt

If you can make soft cheeses, you can make yoghurt* and other curded milks. They are all made in much the same way. Only the organisms which make the curd differ.

Yoghurt is the kind of curded milk we know best and use most often, apart from the soft curd cheeses. We use cow's or goat's milk for both. But instead of the *Strep. Lactis* which sets the cheese curds, yoghurts are set by the organisms called *Lactobacillus bulgaricus* and *Strepococcus thermophilus,* with help from *Lactobacillus acidophilus.* So if you buy or keep yoghurt starter culture and cheese starter culture in similar bottles, take care to label them clearly. Some yoghurt curds make good cheese (page 71), but cheese curds can never make yoghurts.

Unless you want to make yoghurt cheese, there is only one other real difference between preparing yoghurt curds and soft cheese curds; you do not drain them. Yoghurts used for any purpose except cheese still hold their whey.

Yoghurt is made and eaten in many parts of the world, and has many names; most of them are very similar. So, depending on where it comes from, you may see it named:

---

*In Britain, one should, strictly, use the spelling 'yoghourt' for the commercially made product and 'yogurt' for the home-made variety.

Yoghurt	Joghurt
Yogurt	Jogurt
Yoghourt	Kiselo mieko
Yaourti	Prostokvasha
Yaourt	Mast
Yourt	Madzoon
Yogur	Laban zabadi.

You can buy any of these to eat as yoghurt or to use as a starter for making your own. They all contain the yoghurt-making organisms (about 200 million of them per cubic centimetre).

It is useful to remember this because some of the yoghurts taste and look very different. We in Britain like mild-flavoured yoghurt compared with most people on the Continent, while in the East, yoghurt usually has a still more acid flavour. Some peoples, such as the Danes, prefer thin yoghurt and others like it almost as thick as blancmange; in India, a firm, even dryer, crumbly yoghurt is made by squeezing the curds in a cloth.

Note these differences if you come across foreign yoghurts; because, if you want to try a foreign recipe using yoghurt, you must make or buy the right kind, to make a successful dish. A thin, acid yoghurt will not give the same result as a thick, bland, sponge-like one.

It is also useful to remember the various names and different types of yoghurt to avoid confusing them with other cultured milks which you may come across here or on holiday abroad. Most of these are very like yoghurt in taste, looks and smell, and are just as nourishing, but they are set by different organisms and cannot be used to start home-made yoghurt. Some of the names you may come across are: dahi (India); fiili, fillbunke and filmjolk (Scandinavia); kéfir, koumiss (Russia); leben (Turkey, Egypt); suurmelk (Norway); and Ymer (Denmark).

Some of the yoghurts, like these other cultured milks, are thicker than others because a different type of milk is used to set them. In Britain, only cow's or goat's milk is used. But around the Mediterranean, sheep's milk yoghurt is often made, and in North Africa and India, water buffalo milk is used. If you want to try making one of these foreign yoghurts, you cannot get exactly the same flavour by using cow's or goat's milk, but you can make a thick acid curd for foreign dishes which need it very easily. The following ways can be used to thicken the yoghurt:

- make it partly or wholly with skim milk, dried skim milk powder or evaporated milk with 25% less water than usual
- boil the milk down to about two-thirds of its volume before making the yoghurt
- incubate the yoghurt for longer than usual before cooling and storing it; this makes it more acid too
- leave the yoghurt for some time in the refrigerator before using it; this also makes it more acid
- boil the yoghurt to make the curd draw together
- boil the yoghurt, then hang it in a cloth to drain.

The third and fourth ways above raise two others. Unless you want an acid yoghurt, take care not to put in too much starter, and remember to take the yoghurt out of its incubator or out of storage at the right time, and use it. Yoghurt needs so little attention compared with even simple cheeses that it is easy to forget it needs any care at all. But it gets more acid all the time. So, if you want a bland yoghurt, say for a creamy sweet or a dessert cheese, do not leave it incubated or in the refrigerator too long. The yoghurt will come to no harm if you do. But it will not be the product you need, and your sweet dish or cheese may be sour and a failure.

Yoghurt starter culture, like yoghurt for eating, becomes more acid all the time, as it ages. The organisms in it soon convert their nutrients into acid, and need a new source of food; they also multiply very quickly and become too crowded. So you will need to innoculate new bottles of starter culture regularly and often, once you have your first or 'mother' culture.

You can buy your first lot of live starter culture from a laboratory, just as you can buy cheese starter culture (page 72). Alternatively, you can use a little commercial natural yoghurt from a carton. Do not bother to search out a yoghurt labelled as 'live yoghurt'. All yoghurts are 'live'. But do inspect the carton to make sure that the yoghurt is not pasteurised, and that it is not old stock. Only buy it if it is date-stamped with a 'sell by . . .' date still some time ahead, so that you know it is still quite young. Old stock may already be weak and unfit to act as a starter.

When you get your 'mother' culture, prepare at least two bottles of sterile milk to make your own 'follow-on' starter culture immediately. Laboratory starter culture is expensive, and may be difficult to get just when you want it. Commercial yoghurt is also expensive compared with your own. Both have a short life too. A bottle of any starter culture ready for use only lasts about two months, if as long; a carton of commercial yoghurt may only last a week in good condition. You can soon tell when it is failing. If it takes more than six hours to set new yoghurt, it is weak and should be replaced.

To prepare your sterile milk and innoculate it with the 'mother' starter culture, you will need the same equipment as for innoculating milk with cheese starter culture. This consists of:

■ bottles with screw-on caps for the sterile milk
■ a saucepan to boil the milk in
■ a rack, trivet or cloth to put in the saucepan
■ the live starter culture
■ a naked flame, e.g. the burner on a gas cooker or a candle.

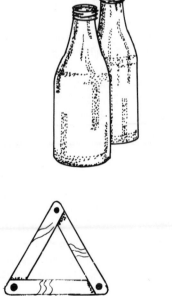

Treat all this equipment as described on page 18 above, to make sure that it is sterile. This is even more important when innoculating milk for yoghurt than when innoculating it for making cheese. Yoghurt-making bacteria are delicate and easily destroyed.

Innoculate your two (or more) bottles of sterile milk in exactly the same way as cheese starter culture (pages 19–20). If you use a laboratory 'mother' culture, follow the manufacturer's directions as to how much of it to add to the milk. If you use commercial yoghurt, use 1 or 2 × 15 ml spoons (1 or 2 tablespoons) for each $\frac{1}{2}$ litre (1 pint) milk. Incubate one bottle of the newly-innoculated milk, and freeze the second and any others, to make sure of your follow-on supply. Remember that bottles of milk for freezing should be only half full.

To incubate the newly-innoculated milk, you must keep the bottle at a temperature of about 45°C (110°F) for 3–4 hours. Put the innoculated bottle into warm water, at a temperature of 46°C (114°–115°F) for about ten minutes, warming the water up if required until the milk has adjusted to this temperature. Use a dairy thermometer to test the temperature of the water. When the milk is warm place the bottle in a wide-necked thermos flask.

Pour the water at 46°C (114°–115°F) into the flask, stopper the flask, and leave for three hours.

At the end of this time, check whether the contents have set or coagulated. If they have, refrigerate the bottle until you need to use it. If the milk is still liquid, re-warm the bottle to 45°C (110°F) as above, and put it back in the flask for another hour. Check again, and repeat the process if necessary. Give the culture up to six hours to set. If it is still liquid at the end of that time, it is too weak to use, and you must throw it away and start again.

If you have to throw it away, remember to discard any frozen starter culture which you innoculated at the same time; it will be just as weak. You will be wasting freezer-space by leaving it in the freezer; and you may forget, later, that it is a 'dud', and try to thaw and incubate it with disappointing results.

Once you have your starter culture, you are ready to make yoghurt for eating. You do this in much the same way as you incubate the starter culture. It is extremely easy, provided you make sure that your equipment is sterile, and that you have adequate space at a constant temperature of about 46°C (114°F) to incubate the yoghurt.

Equipment:

The equipment you need will vary slightly, depending on whether you want to make yoghurt in bulk, for use by a commune or for sale, or only want to make enough for everyday use by a small family. It will vary, too, according to the way you incubate it. But you will need, most, or all, of the following.

For making in bulk

- a large pan, double boiler or bucket
- a dairy thermometer
- a large whisk
- a 500 ml (1 pint) jug
- a 500 ml (1 pint) bowl
- long-handled spoons
- containers with lids for the prepared yoghurt
- wooden incubating box with a lid, fully lined with polystyrene ceiling or wall tiles
- a warmed blanket.

For home use

- a small pan or double boiler
- a jug
- a dairy thermometer
- a whisk
- 2 or 3 1 litre ($1\frac{1}{2}$–$1\frac{3}{4}$ pint) bowls
- a small bowl
- spoons
- a warmed blanket or a wide-necked thermos flask and a funnel
- a container with a lid for the pre-pared yoghurt.

Sterilise this equipment in the same way as for cheese-making. Boil as much of it as you can, and scrub the rest with very hot water (no detergent or soap). Turn bowls upside down, and cover tools, etc. with clean boiled cloths until they are needed. Yoghurt-making bacteria are easily destroyed by invaders, especially by yeasts.

For this reason, scald (or for thicker yoghurt, boil) the milk you intend to use. Pasteurising is not enough. Any milk except dried skim milk powder, canned evaporated milk, sterilised and UHT milk should be scalded almost to boiling point or boiled, and then cooled to the temperature given in the following recipes.

To make Yoghurt in Bulk

4½ litres (1 gallon) full cream
4½ litres (1 gallon) full cream, partly
   skimmed or skimmed milk
200–300 g (8–12 oz.) dried skim
   milk powder for thick yoghurt
   (optional)
125 ml (¼ pint) starter culture

Start heating the milk gently, and whisk in the milk powder if used when the temperature of the liquid milk reaches 45°C (110°F). Heat the milk to at least 82°C (180°F), then stand the pan in a sink of cold water, to cool the milk as quickly as possible to 46°C (115°F). Using a sterile jug, transfer 250 ml (½ pint) of the cooled milk to a bowl. Mix in the 125 ml (¼ pint) starter. Return the milk to the pan, and mix it into the remaining milk well. Transfer the startered milk carefully, without jolting it, to sterilised containers with lids.

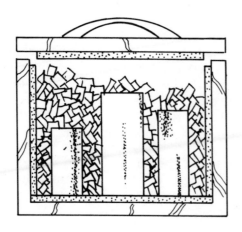

Place the containers in the lined incubating box, and surround them with tightly packed polystyrene chips. Close the lid securely, and cover with a warmed blanket for 3–4 hours until a firm curd has formed. Remove from the box as soon as you find the milk has curded; do not over-incubate.

Refrigerate the yoghurt for 10–12 hours. Then flavour if desired (page 61), and transfer carefully to small containers with lids, for use, storage or sale.

———

It is not practical to use an unusual milk mixture to make yoghurt in bulk. But if you make it for home use, you can use any of the following mixtures. Each will give you a slightly different yoghurt, more or less rich, thick or thin. Try out the ones which are practical for you to use, and find the one you like best for regular use:

- raw fresh milk boiled for five minutes and cooled to 46°C (115°F) (for average yoghurt)
- pasteurised milk, boiled and cooled as above (for average yoghurt)
- homogenised milk, boiled and cooled as above (for average yoghurt)
- a mixture of raw, pasteurised and homogenised milk, boiled and cooled as above (for average yoghurt)
- sterilised milk (for a thin yoghurt)
- UHT milk (for a fairly thin yoghurt, unless boiled and cooled as above)
- any of the milks above, partly or wholly skimmed (for thicker yoghurt)
- boiled or sterilised milk + 100 g (4 oz.) dried skimmed milk powder per 480 ml (1 pint) milk (for thick yoghurt)

- 75 g (3 oz.) dried skimmed milk powder + 480–500 ml (1 pint) boiled and cooled water (for thick yoghurt)
- any mixture of the milks above.

Besides a choice of milks, you can choose one of several ways in which to incubate the yoghurt, since it will not take up much space. One way which is often used is to wrap the container in a warmed blanket and let it rest in an airing cupboard with an even temperature, on a night storage heater, or on a bed with an electric blanket, switched on to give a low heat. Another way is to use an electric yoghurt – making machine, such as the one shown on the jacket. A third way is to incubate the yoghurt in a wide-necked thermos flask.

Choose whichever is most practical for you. Remember that the surrounding temperature needs to be slightly warmer than the yoghurt itself.

To Make Average or Thin Yoghurt for Home Use (blanket method)

500 ml (1 pint) of any milk or mixture of milks from any of the first six above
2 × 15 ml level spoons (2 level tablespoons) starter culture or natural yoghurt, bought or home-made

Boil and cool the milk if necessary as described above. Transfer a small quantity to a sterile bowl, and whisk in the culture or yoghurt. Whisk the mixture into the remaining milk, making sure that it is blended in thoroughly. Transfer to a sterile container with a lid, wrap in a warmed blanket and keep at a temperature of 43°C (110°F) for 3–4 hours in one of the ways described above. Then check whether a curd has formed. If not, incubate for up to six hours, but no longer (see page 58 above).

When the curd has formed, let the container cool at room temperature, then refrigerate for 10–12 hours. Flavour if desired (page 61), and store in the refrigerator, well covered, until required.

Note: if using culture from a large bottle or yoghurt from a large carton, take it from the centre of the container where the bacteria are most likely to be well mixed and active.

To Make Thick Yoghurt for Home Use (thermos method)

75 g (3 oz.) dried skimmed milk powder
480 ml (1 pint) water or milk mixture which gives a thick curd
2 × 15 ml spoons (2 tablespoons) low fat natural yoghurt

Place the skimmed milk powder in a 700 ml (1½ pint) bowl. Bring the water to the boil, and boil for about two minutes. Mix enough water with the milk powder to make a smooth paste. Then gradually add the rest of the water, beating out any lumps. Cool the mixture to 45°C (115°F).

While the milk cools, boil a kettle of water and rinse out a wide-necked thermos flask with it. (Do not use a narrow-necked flask; the yoghurt curd will break up when you try to get it out.) Pour some of the water through a metal funnel too.

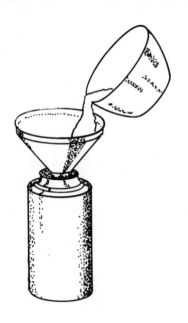

When the milk has cooled to 46°C (115°F) mix in the low-fat yoghurt and stir well to blend the two thoroughly. Pour the mixture into the flask through the funnel, then stopper the flask securely. Leave in a reasonably warm place for 3–4 hours for a bland, fairly thick yoghurt. Leave for up to eight hours for a really thick, more acid yoghurt.

Transfer the curd when formed to a sterile container with a lid. Cool at room temperature, then refrigerate for 10–12 hours. Flavour if desired (page 61). Cover closely and store in the refrigerator until required.

Processing Yoghurt

Whether or not you process yoghurt after making it will depend on:

- how much yoghurt you make (it is seldom worth making less than 500 ml (1 pt.)
- how much yoghurt your family or group eats as it is
- whether it is good yoghurt for your purpose (if, for instance, you make a thin acid yoghurt by mistake when you want to use it instead of sweet thick cream you may have to find an alternative use for it)
- whether you think yoghurt a 'wonder food' for health; see page 54. If you do, you will want to use it in every way you can, cooked or as it is, chilled, hot, etc.

Yoghurt is excellent as it is for many purposes, but there are limits to the quantity which even an addict can eat in the course of a day; and since it gets more acid as it ages, a spare bowlful can become unpleasant to eat even in a refrigerator, unless eaten quite soon. So you may easily find you need to process it quickly for use in other ways, either by flavouring it or cooking with it.

Yoghurt teams well with many flavourings and additions. There are only two snags. It is usually unwise to add a flavouring to it before incubating it, because yoghurt-making bacteria may be upset or made impotent by it; and you cannot stir it in afterwards if you want the yoghurt to be thick and curdy, like junket, because stirring makes it liquid and smooth. Any solid additions may tend to sink to the bottom, too. So a certain amount of care is needed when you want to use a flavouring.

As a rule, yoghurt which has become liquid by stirring remains creamy and firms up again if it stands for a short while, especially if you drain off some of the whey which separates from the curd as you break it up. So any stirred-in flavouring should be added ahead of the time when the yoghurt will be eaten or cooked if you want it thick and firm. Remember, though, that the yoghurt may get more acid even within a few hours and add the right quantity of flavouring to allow for it.

Do not over-flavour, however. Any flavouring, savoury or sweet, should 'marry with' the yoghurt's natural flavour, not try to overwhelm it. The only exception is when the yoghurt has become too acid to be pleasant eaten alone. In this case, you may need to hide some of its acidity although you can never overcome it entirely and should not try to. Choose a flavouring which needs an acid 'background' instead.

There are three ways of adding a flavouring to yoghurt. You can:

- infuse it in the yoghurt
- mix it into the yoghurt to flavour it evenly throughout
- add it in grains, shreds, etc., which stay distinct from the yoghurt itself.

Infusion

In this case, you put a solid, highly-flavoured ingredient into the yoghurt for a time, then remove it before using the yoghurt. This is the way which disturbs the yoghurt least, if you want it to keep its consistency. For instance, stick a bay leaf into the yoghurt, leaving its stalk above the surface, and simply withdraw it when you want to use the yoghurt; or put one or two whole cleaned spring onions into the yoghurt with their green stems sticking out in the same way. A peeled garlic clove or similar small item can be stuck on a point of a skewer, to save hunting for it with a teaspoon when you want to remove it.

Mixing

Powdered or liquid ingredients and essences, are usually mixed into the yoghurt to flavour it evenly. There is really no way to do this but to stir them in thoroughly, let the yoghurt become creamy, then leave it to firm up again. You do not want, suddenly, to taste an undiluted spot of soy sauce, or grains of curry powder, in semi-mixed yoghurt.

Solid Ingredients

Minced, shredded or minutely diced items can be added to yoghurt with-without disturbing it much if you scatter them on the surface, then prod them with the point of a knife or a skewer to push them below the surface of the yoghurt. If they have any liquid with them, however, e.g. oil with chopped anchovies or olives, or juice with shreds of canned pineapple, it will lie on the surface and you will have to stir it in gently. Again, a skewer is a good tool to do it with if you do not

want to disturb the yoghurt overmuch.

Yoghurt goes well with so many different flavourings that it would be impossible to give you a complete list. On page 64, is just a short list of some of the more common ones, both savoury and sweet. Use it as a 'signpost' to help you think of others; a great many cook-books give recipes which contain yoghurt with flavourings.

Any of these flavourings and many others, can be added to yoghurt which will be eaten by itself or will be used uncooked as part of a salad or dessert. Almost any of them can be added to yoghurt intended for a cooked dish too. But as a rule, yoghurt is added un-flavoured to cooked dishes, since any flavourings can just as easily be put in the dish separately. (There is no reason why you should not add pre-flavoured yoghurt to a cooked dish, though, for instance, if you have some to use up.)

Once you have started making yoghurt, you will certainly want to use it in cooked dishes sometimes (see page 61). This is not difficult, but, like flavouring yoghurt, it needs a little care. This is because European yoghurt curdles if it is heated quickly, is boiled or cooked for long; the dish then looks speckled instead of smooth and creamy, although the food value and flavour are not spoiled.

The easiest way to avoid curdling the yoghurt is to choose recipes in which it is only added at the end of the cooking time. But if you need to add it sooner, you must either mix it with some kind of flour or with egg just before you use it, or it must be 'stabilised' ahead of time.

'Stabilising' the yoghurt serves two important purposes, besides preventing it curdling. First, it makes the yoghurt last, unchanged for up to two weeks in refrigerator. Second, it thickens the yoghurt. This is often helpful and may be essential, if you want to use it:

- instead of cream
- in a casserole dish or 'bake', or in any dish which needs a thick sauce
- for making cakes or pastry
- with thin liquid flavourings such as fruit juice
- in most foreign dishes.

It can also help you hide the fact, if you need to, that a particular batch of yoghurt has not been fully successful and has turned out too thin for your family's usual taste.

To Stabilise or Thicken Yoghurt

For each 1 litre (1¾ pt.) yoghurt use:

1 large egg white
or
1 slightly rounded 15 ml spoon (tablespoon) cornflour and a little cold milk
Salt to taste

Beat the egg white until liquid or mix the cornflour with enough milk to make a very smooth paste. Add a very little salt (only a few grains if the yoghurt is for a sweet dish). Beat the yoghurt in a large saucepan until liquid and smooth and add the egg white or cornflour paste gradually. Then heat the yoghurt gently, and bring it slowly to the boil, stirring steadily, in one direction only. As soon as it bubbles, reduce the heat to as low as possible. Simmer, uncovered, for about 10 minutes until the yoghurt has the consistency of thick cream. Cool at room temperature. Cover and store in the refrigerator for up to two weeks.

If you have no stabilised yoghurt ready, but need thick yoghurt in a cooked dish, mix 500 ml (1 pt.) yoghurt with 4 × 5 ml spoons (4 teaspoons) plain flour, cornflour or potato flour, or with one whole egg or two egg yolks, just before using it. Which you use will depend on whether it is easier to add a paste or a liquid to the particular cooked dish and whether you want to make it richer (with the egg). In both cases, blend the yoghurt with the extra ingredient thoroughly, to get rid of lumps or any streaks of egg before you use it.

If you stabilise your spare yoghurt, you may avoid having to cook with it in order to use it quickly. However, having a stock of thick, stabilised yoghurt also gives you a much wider choice of cooked recipes to use if you need to. So it helps you to make the very most of your yoghurt, by using it in ways you really enjoy.

In the next section, you will find some of the ways in which you can use both thin and thick yoghurt, to make the most of it. It gives, first, ideas for using uncooked yoghurt and then some recipes for using it in cooked dishes. Look at the yoghurt recipes in other sections of the book too.

Yoghurt Flavourings and Seasonings

Infused Flavourings

- bay leaf
- slice of onion (on skewer)
- garlic clove (on skewer)
- spring onion (leave stems sticking out of the yoghurt)
- piece of horseradish (on skewer)
- sprig of mint, rosemary, basil or other fresh herb (for a delicate herb flavour—leave stems sticking out of the yoghurt)
- strongly-spiced salami slice or smoked sausage slice (on skewer)
- piece of stem ginger (on skewer)
- cinnamon stick (for a light cinnamon flavour—leave one end sticking out of the yoghurt)
- stick of peppermint rock (leave one end sticking out of the yoghurt).

Flavourings and Seasonings Mixed In

- salt
- pepper, black or white, Cayenne, paprika
- ground cinnamon
- grated nutmeg
- ground allspice
- other ground spice, any kind, to suit flavour of yoghurt, e.g. cardomum, clove, ginger
- curry powder
- chilli powder
- turmeric
- sesame seeds
- dill, fennel or other herb seeds
- crushed dried thyme, mint, marjoram, sage or any other herb to suit flavour of yoghurt
- Worcestershire sauce
- soy sauce
- vinegar, wine, malt or spiced anchovy essence
- tomato ketchup, mushroom, ketchup, etc.
- canned condensed soup
- tomato juice, purée or paste
- Harvey's, HP or a similar sauce (avoid any product containing yeast extract)
- cider
- wine, red or white
- fine sugar, e.g. icing, caster, granulated or soft brown (coarse sugar crystals, e.g. Demerara may half-melt into minute pools of liquid sugar, giving the yoghurt a speckled appearance)

- vermouth, any kind
- spirits, e.g. whisky
- grated orange or lemon peel
- liqueur, any kind, to suit flavour of yoghurt
- strained fruit juice, any kind, to suit flavour of yoghurt
- honey, golden syrup, molasses, maple syrup
- grated chocolate
- cocoa powder with sugar
- instant coffee powder with sugar
- vanilla essence
- lemon essence
- other fruit flower or liqueur essence, e.g. cherry, rose, brandy.

Solid Flavouring Ingredients

(minced, chopped, shredded or finely diced)

- pickles
- olives
- green peppers
- carrot
- cucumber
- onion
- dill (stem)
- fennel (bulb)
- other firm salad ingredient (avoid shredded lettuce, chopped beetroot, tomato)
- anchovy fillets
- smoked haddock, cod and similar fish
- canned sardine, herring, mackerel and similar fish
- pickled fish
- shrimps and other shellfish including smoked shellfish (e.g. oysters)
- well-flavoured meat, e.g. ham
- smoked meat, any kind, to suit flavour of yoghurt
- sausage, e.g. salami, to suit flavour of yoghurt
- grated cheese, any kind
- scrambled or hard-boiled egg
- canned fruit, any kind (avoid fresh fruit and nuts unless the yoghurt will be eaten at once)
- dessicated coconut
- candied fruit peel, any kind, e.g. mixed chopped peel
- dried fruit, any kind
- soft sweets, e.g. peppermint creams, fudge (avoid toffees, caramels, hard clear gums)
- crushed nut brittle
- broken meringues.

Making the Most of Yoghurt

Ideas for Using Uncooked Yoghurt

- Use yoghurt as a dish in itself. Top or mix it with a small quantity of:

- chopped salad ingredients, e.g.

  watercress
  cucumber
  olives
  spring onion
  capers
  gherkins
  green pepper
  cooked green peas

- spicy ingredients, e.g.

  pickles
  paprika
  ketchup
  crumbed stock cube
  bottled sauce
  chutney
  curry powder
  anchovy essence or sauce
  tomato purée or paste
  prepared mustard

- chopped 'protein' ingredients, e.g.

  scrambled egg
  cooked bacon
  ham
  any soft cheese
  (grated) hard cheese
  cooked chicken
  hard-boiled egg
  cooked or smoked sausage
  smoked fish (raw, e.g. mackerel)
  smoked fish (cooked, e.g. haddock)
  canned sardine or herring, drained
  canned or bottled shellfish, drained
  anchovy fillets

- chopped sweet ingredients, e.g.

  well-drained canned fruit
  crystallised ginger or other fruit
  chocolate vermicelli
  (crushed) chocolate flake
  (coarsely grated) bitter chocolate
  candied fruit or peel
  glacé fruits
  raisins or sultanas
  dessert dates
  (crushed) nut brittle
  (crushed) peppermint rock
  marshmallows

- sweet sauce items, e.g.

  seedless jam or jelly (blackcurrant
    is very good)
  Melba sauce
  instant dessert whip
  canned strained baby food
  honey
  golden syrup
  molasses
  maple syrup
  fruit purée or sauce
  instant coffee powder and sugar.

- Use yoghurt instead of cream, soured cream or milk, e.g.

  on breakfast cereals
  on stewed fruit

on rice puddings and hot steamed
   sponge puddings
in dips
in spreads and sandwich fillings
in salad dressings
in cream sauces
in other thick savoury sauces
in syllabubs
in fruit fools
in layered creamy desserts
in milk shakes
with ice cream
for making scones and drop scones
for making cakes and pastry
on cheesecakes
in beef Stroganoff
in mayonnaise sauces
as a 'binder' for rissole mixtures
in fritter batters
for making pancakes
in pasta dishes
in stuffings for vegetables or meats.

■ Use yoghurt as a topping, e.g.

on muesli
on hot puddings (sprinkled with
   sugar)
on flans and tarts (sprinkled with
   sugar)
on cold desserts, e.g. trifle
on crystallised ginger
on vegetables
on pasta dishes (sprinkled with
   grated cheese) and pancakes
on chicken salad
on cold fish salads
on cold vegetable salads
on 'bakes'
on rich brown casseroles
on jugged hare and salmi of game
   or pigeon
on braised meats
on baked lamb.

Here are some particular ideas to try:
■ add thick natural yoghurt to a
  chicken casserole just before serving.
  Do not stir it in; the white swirls on
  the sauce look tempting
■ add natural yoghurt in the same way
  to an ox-tail stew or any rich brown
  stew
■ use natural yoghurt instead of soft
  cheese or butter in baked potatoes in
  their jackets
■ stir natural yoghurt into any sauce
  for chicken, fish or veal just before
  serving, especially one flavoured
  with lemon
■ serve natural yoghurt, well chilled,
  as a dessert in stemmed individual
  glasses with a thin layer of honey on
  each helping
■ serve alternate layers of natural
  yoghurt and jam in glasses as above,
  well chilled. Top with shortbread
  crumbs (choose a red jam; the
  stripes of red and white look attractive through the glass)
■ mix yoghurt with marmalade, chill,
  and serve in individual stemmed
  glasses. Top each helping with
  toasted coarse oatmeal and brown
  sugar.

Yoghurt Refresher

Makes 4 helpings.

500 ml (1 pint) natural yoghurt
500 ml (1 pint) orange or pineapple
   juice
1–2 drops Angostura bitters

Stir the yoghurt until smooth. Mix in
the juice and bitters. Chill well, and
serve in chilled glasses.

Savoury White Sauce

35 g (1½ oz.) butter
25 g (1 oz.) flour
250 ml (½ pint) milk
100 ml (4 fl. oz.) natural yoghurt
Salt and pepper to taste

Melt the butter and stir in the flour. Add the milk gradually, stirring all the time. Bring slowly to the boil, still stirring continuously. When the sauce thickens slightly, stir in the yoghurt. Season to taste. Serve hot.

Yoghurt Crust for Savoury 'Bakes'

250 ml (½ pint) thick natural yoghurt
2 eggs
25 g (1 oz.) flour
Salt and pepper to taste
1–2 × 15 ml spoons (1–2 tablespoons) grated cheese

Stir the yoghurt until smooth. Beat the eggs until liquid, and mix in the flour, smoothing out any lumps. Mix the egg-flour mixture into the yoghurt. Season well, mix in cheese and pour over the dish. Bake at 190°C (375°F), Gas 5 for 20–35 minutes until golden-brown.

This crust makes a good topping for any gratin. It is also a good way to re-heat cold cooked leftover pasta, or cooked braised leeks, cabbage or spinach as a main dish.

Yoghurt Salad Dressing

200 ml (8 fl. oz.) natural yoghurt
A few drops strained lemon juice
Salt and pepper to taste

½ × 2.5 ml spoon (¼ teaspoon) freshly squeezed garlic or garlic salt (optional)

Mix all the ingredients together thoroughly. Serve on salads.

Variation:

Spanish Salad Dressing

Add to the mixture above:

1 × 5 ml spoon (1 teaspoon) finely-chopped gherkin
1 × 5 ml spoon (1 teaspoon) finely-chopped pimento
1 × 5 ml spoon (1 teaspoon) finely-chopped chives
1 × 2.5 ml spoon (½ teaspoon) celery or dill seed

Cole Slaw

400–500 g (¾–1 lb.) white cabbage
2 × 15 ml spoons (2 tablespoons) vinegar or lemon juice
125 ml (¼ pint) natural yoghurt
50 ml (2 fl. oz.) mayonnaise
2 small carrots, coarsely grated
Salt to taste
Sugar to taste

Shred the cabbage and mix with the carrot. Mix together the yoghurt, mayonnaise and vinegar or lemon juice. Season to taste. Mix well with the cabbage and carrot. Chill before serving.

Yoghurt, Potato and Watercress Salad

4 large potatoes or 12 new potatoes

1 × 15 ml spoon (1 tablespoon)
  salad oil
3 × 15 ml spoons (3 tablespoons)
  mild vinegar
3 × 15 ml spoons (3 tablespoons)
  finely-chopped celery
2 hard-boiled eggs, chopped
1 small onion, chopped
Salt and pepper to taste
125 ml ($\frac{1}{4}$ pint) natural yoghurt
100 ml (4 fl. oz.) mayonnaise
Grapefruit segments to decorate
Watercress sprigs to decorate

Bake large potatoes in their skins or boil new ones. Cool, peel and dice potatoes, cover with the oil and vinegar and allow to stand for one hour at room temperature. Add the celery, eggs and onion, and season to taste. Mix the yoghurt with the mayonnaise, and mix well with the potato dish. Decorate with grapefruit segments and watercress just before serving.

Watercress Soup

Makes 4 helpings

100 g (4 oz.) butter or margarine
50 g (2 oz.) flour
500 ml (1 pint) chicken stock
125 ml ($\frac{1}{4}$ pint) single cream
50 g (2 oz.) minced onion
3 bunches watercress
Salt and pepper to taste
Natural yoghurt as required

Melt 75 g (3 oz.) of the fat in a heavy pan, and stir in the flour. Cook for 1–2 minutes without colouring. Remove the pan from the heat, and gradually stir in the stock and cream, beating out any lumps. Replace over heat, and

bring gently to the boil, stirring continuously. Simmer for three minutes. Remove from the heat and leave aside. Melt the remaining fat, and simmer the onions until cooked. Wash and chop the watercress finely, using about half the stems. Reserve a few choice leaves for garnishing. Add the chopped watercress to the onions, cover the pan, and cook gently for about five minutes. Add to the soup and rub the whole mixture through a sieve (or process in an electric blender). Re-heat, and season well. Pour into heated soup cups. Add a 'floater' of natural yoghurt to each cup, and top with watercress leaves. Serve hot with Buttermilk Puffs, page 53.

Clear Tomato Soup

Makes 4 helpings

1$\frac{1}{4}$ litres (2 pints) clear stock
4 large ripe tomatoes, cut in quarters
A few drops tarragon vinegar
A few drops lemon juice
Sprinkling of salt and pepper
A drop of two of red colouring
2 × 15 ml spoons (2 tablespoons)
  white wine
Pinch of sugar
1 egg white and shell
1 × 5 ml spoon (1 teaspoon)
  arrowroot
Natural yoghurt as required
Sprinkling of crushed dried basil

Pour the stock into a saucepan, and add the tomatoes, vinegar, lemon juice and sprinkling of salt and pepper. Simmer for 45 minutes. Strain into a clean pan and stir in the red colouring, wine and sugar. Add the egg white and shell. Simmer for a further 15 minutes. Lay a clean cloth in a sieve placed over a basin, and strain the soup into it. Adjust the seasoning if required. Mix the arrowroot with a little cold water, and add to the soup. Re-heat gently without boiling until the arrowroot is transparent. Pour into heated serving bowls, float a generous dollop of yoghurt on top of each and sprinkle with the basil.

Note: use the egg yolk to make a firm custard with extra yoghurt. Allow it to get cold, then cut into small dice to garnish the soup.

Green Summer Soup (Chilled)

Makes 4 helpings

150 g (6 oz.) raw potato
100 g (4 oz.) onion, skinned
3–4 lettuce leaves
250 g (10 oz.) frozen peas
500 ml (1 pint) chicken stock
Strip of lemon peel
250 ml ($\frac{1}{2}$ pint) natural yoghurt
Salt and pepper to taste
Pinch of sugar
5 cm (2 in.) cucumber

Peel a slice of potato, slice the onion and shred the lettuce leaves. Place them in a saucepan with most of the peas, the stock and the lemon peel. Heat to simmering point, and simmer for 10–15 minutes. Discard the peel. Rub the mixture through a sieve (or process in an electric blender). Stir the yoghurt until smooth, and add most of it to the soup; keep back 4 × 15 ml spoons (4 tablespoons). Chill the soup for 4–6 hours.

Before serving, season the soup well. Dice the cucumber finely. Divide the cucumber dice and the reserved peas between four chilled soup cups. Pour in the soup, and put a spoonful of yoghurt on each helping.

Bacon and Corn Flan

Makes 4–5 helpings

150–175 g (6–7 oz.) short crust
   pastry
100 g (4 oz.) cold cooked bacon
   joint
2 eggs
1 × 175 g (7 oz.) can sweet corn
   kernels
125 ml ($\frac{1}{4}$ pint) thick natural yoghurt
1 × 15 ml spoon (1 tablespoon)
   chopped parsley
Good pinch of dry mustard
Salt and pepper to taste

Line a greased 20 cm (8 in.) flan ring or sandwich tin with the pastry. Chill. Chop the bacon into small dice. Beat the eggs. Mix in the bacon dice, sweet corn kernels including any juice in the can, the yoghurt, parsley and seasonings. Pour the mixture into the flan case. Bake at 190°C (375°F), Gas 5 for 40–45 minutes, or until the filling is slightly browned and firm in the centre.

Moussaka

Makes four helpings

2 skinned aubergines
25 g (1 oz.) butter
2 cloves garlic, peeled and crushed
2 medium-sized onions, sliced

480 g (1 lb.) cooked, cubed lamb
350 g (14 oz.) canned tomatoes
1 × 5 ml spoon (1 teaspoon) dried
   oregano
1 × 2.5 ml spoon ($\frac{1}{2}$ teaspoon) dried
   basil
1 × 5 ml spoon (1 teaspoon) fresh
   or dried rosemary
Salt and pepper to taste
250 ml ($\frac{1}{2}$ pint) natural yoghurt
3 egg yolks
1 × 15 ml spoon (1 tablespoon)
   grated Gruyère cheese
1 × 15 ml spoon (1 tablespoon)
   flaked butter

Slice the aubergines and blanch in boiling water for two minutes. Drain well. Melt the 25 g (1 oz.) butter in a flameproof casserole, add the garlic and onions and the drained aubergine slices and mix together. Cook gently for 10 minutes, turning the mixture over from time to time. Add the lamb, tomatoes, herbs and seasoning. Cover, and cook gently for a further 10 minutes. While cooking, pour the yoghurt into a small saucepan and beat it well. Beat the egg yolks until liquid, mix them with the yoghurt and cook over the lowest possible heat, stirring continuously, until the mixture thickens Pour the mixture over the casserole. Sprinkle with the cheese and dot with butter flakes. Cook, uncovered, at 180°C (350°F) Gas 4 for 30 minutes. Serve hot, with a salad which includes chilled (slightly acid) soft cheese.

Brandied Grapefruit Dessert

Makes 4 helpings

2 grapefruit
125 ml ($\frac{1}{4}$ pint) natural yoghurt

2 × 15 ml spoons (2 tablespoons)
   brandy
2 × 15 ml spoons Demerara sugar
2 × 5 ml spoons (2 teaspoons)
   redcurrant jelly

Cut the grapefruit in half and cut the flesh of the segments free of the skin. Remove the flesh to a bowl and discard the skins, pips and any loose pith. Mix together the grapefruit flesh, yoghurt and brandy. Spoon the mixture into the grapefruit skins and level the tops. Sprinkle with the Demerara sugar. Place under a hot grill, until the sugar bubbles. Place 1 × 2.5 ml spoon ($\frac{1}{2}$ teaspoon) jelly in the centre of each half grapefruit. Serve hot, with shortbread.

Strawberry Joy

Makes 4 helpings

1 × 425 g (15 oz.) can strawberries
1 × 10 ml spoon (1 dessertspoon)
   gelatine
250 ml ($\frac{1}{2}$ pint) natural yoghurt
A few drops lemon juice (optional)
Chilled whipped cream as required
Toasted almonds to decorate
   (optional)

Drain the syrup from the fruit and add enough water to the syrup to make 250 ml ($\frac{1}{2}$ pint) liquid. Place 4 × 15 ml spoons (4 tablespoons) syrup into a small heatproof basin and sprinkle the gelatine on top, to soften. When soft, stand the basin in simmering water, and stir until the gelatine dissolves. Add the remaining syrup. Stir the yoghurt until smooth and mix with the syrup. Taste and add lemon juice if desired. Refrigerate until on the point of setting.

Fold in the drained fruit and turn into a serving bowl or individual glasses. Top with chilled whipped cream and decorate with toasted almonds if desired.

Blackcurrant Cream Desserts

Makes 4 helpings

125 ml ($\frac{1}{4}$ pint) double cream
125 ml ($\frac{1}{4}$ pint) thick natural yoghurt
100 g (4 oz.) shortbread crumbs
2 × 15 ml spoons (2 tablespoons) caster sugar
1 × 5 ml spoon (1 teaspoon) lemon juice (optional)
1 × 5 ml spoon blackcurrant liqueur (optional)
300–350 g (12–14 oz.) blackcurrant jam

Whip the cream until semi-stiff. Stir the yoghurt until smooth and stir lightly into the cream. Whip again, if required, to make the mixture semi-stiff. Fold in the crumbs and sugar.

Blend the lemon juice and liqueur if used into the jam. Place a layer of jam in each of four tall stemmed flute glasses. Top with a layer of cream mixture. Repeat the layers until the ingredients are used, ending with cream mixture. Decorate with a blob of jam in the centre of each dessert. Chill well before serving.

Yoghurt Cheese or Labna Cheese

Use thick natural yoghurt made by the thermos method (page 59). Pour or spoon it into a square of muslin which has been boiled for 10 minutes and then chilled. Gather up the corners of the muslin to form a bag, and hang it over a bowl for 24–48 hours. Twice during this time, open the bag, and scrape the yoghurt from the sides of the cloth. Mix the firm yoghurt next to the cloth with the softer yoghurt in the centre, and re-hang the bag.

After 48 hours, turn the yoghurt into a bowl and salt it to taste. Cover and store in the refrigerator for not more than seven days.

An excellent, firm cheese for cheesecakes.

Yoghurt Scones

Makes 10–12 scones

200 g (8 oz.) self-raising flour
1 × 2.5 ml spoon ($\frac{1}{2}$ teaspoon) salt
50 g (2 oz.) margarine
4 × 15 ml spoons (4 tablespoons) thick natural yoghurt
4 × 15 ml spoons (4 tablespoons) milk

Sift the flour and salt into a mixing bowl. Rub in the fat until the mixture resembles fine crumbs. Mix the yoghurt and milk together. Mix the dry ingredients to a soft dough with the yoghurt-milk mixture. Cut out scones with a 6 cm ($2\frac{1}{2}$ in.) cutter. Place on a lightly greased baking sheet, and bake at 230°C (450°F), Gas 8, for about 15 minutes or until lightly browned. Serve while still warm, split and filled with soft cheese and redcurrant jelly; or cool, split, toast, and serve with cheese.

Further Reading

The Story of Cheese-Making in Britain, Val Cheke (Routledge and Kegan Paul, 1959)
A Handbook of Dairy Foods for Senior Students (National Dairy Council, 1974)
The Backyard Dairy Book, Street and Singer (Prism Press, 1972) *
Self-Sufficiency, J. and S. Seymour (Faber, 1973) *
Cooking with Yogurt, Cultured Cream and Soft Cheeses, Nilson (Pelham, 1973)
Salute to Cheese, Betty Wason (Ward Lock, 1968)
Cheeses of the World, Simon (Faber, 1965)

Consumer Guidance Organisations

National Dairy Council,
5 John Princes Street,
London, W1

(Consumer Guidance)

National Federation of Women's
   Institutes,
39 Eccleston Square,
London, SW1

(Consumer Guidance)

Small Scale Supplies,
Widdington,
Saffron Walden,
Essex,
CB11 35P

(Domestic home dairying equipment)

Christian Hansen Laboratories Ltd,
476 Basingstoke Road,
Reading, RG2 0QL

(Starters, rennets, colourings, etc.)

Akzo Chemie (UK) Ltd,
12–14 St. Ann's Crescent,
Wandsworth,
London, SW18 2LS

(Non-animal, vegetarian starters,
   rennets, etc.)

Lotus Foods Ltd,
29–31 St. Luke's Mews,
London, W11 1DF

(Vegetarian rennet, stock and other
   flavourings, etc.)